super salads

quadrille

This edition first published in 2007 by **Quadrille Publishing Limited**
Alhambra House, 27-31 Charing Cross Road, London WC2H 0LS

Editorial Director Jane O'Shea
Creative Director Helen Lewis
Editor Laura Herring
Designer Ros Holder
Production Bridget Fish

Text © 2007 Seven Publishing Group
Photography © 2007 Seven Publishing Group
(for a full list of contributors and photographers, see pages 284–5)
Design and layout © 2007 Quadrille Publishing Limited

Most of the material in this volume was previously published in **delicious.**
magazine or **Sainsbury's Magazine** and was provided courtesy of the Seven
Publishing Group.

Cataloguing in Publication Data:
a catalogue record for this book is available from the British Library.

ISBN 978 184400 487 4
Printed in China

Cookery notes
All spoon measures are level unless otherwise stated: 1 teaspoon = 5 ml
spoon; 1 tablespoon = 15 ml spoon. Use fresh herbs unless dried herbs are
suggested. Use sea salt and freshly ground black pepper unless otherwise
stated. Free-range eggs are recommended and large eggs should be used
except where a different size is specified. Recipes which feature raw or
lightly cooked eggs should be avoided by anyone who is pregnant or in
a vulnerable health group.

Contents

Introduction

The salad is one of the most flexible and adaptable dishes, offering the basis for infinite combinations of flavours and ingredients. From the light summer dishes we are familiar with to recipes for warm and hearty meals, the salads in this book cover the whole range – as well as a selection of hot and cold fruit salads.

Super Salads proves there is more to this versatile dish than crisp lettuce and sliced tomato. The recipes here are inventive and diverse making creative use of unexpected ingredients such as duck, pheasant, razor clams and roast lamb.

You'll find Spanish, Italian, Chinese, Thai and British influences vying for your attention, and the recipes are organised into chapters by their main ingredient for easy selection. There is also a final chapter on the techniques of making dressings and mayonnaises with suggestions on what best to pair them with.

From the classic Greek salad, through tempting side-dishes, including a warm barley salad with butternut squash, to twists on traditional favourites and a large selection of substantial main courses, there is something here for every occasion all year round.

salads
starters & light salads

Parma ham, fig & mozzarella salad

Serves 2–3
50g rocket leaves
6 ripe figs
2 x 175g buffalo mozzarella balls
6 slices Parma ham
2 tbsp honey
2 tbsp lemon juice
freshly ground black pepper
2–3 pitta breads

1. Spread the rocket leaves onto a platter. Cut the figs in half and arrange on the leaves.
2. Tear the buffalo mozzarella and add to the platter. Tear the Parma ham slices into strips and arrange on the platter.
3. Mix the honey with the lemon juice and drizzle over the top. Season with black pepper.
4. Pop a few pitta breads in the toaster and serve warm with the salad.

Broad bean, mint & crispy pancetta

Serves 4
12 thin slices pancetta
750g freshly shelled or frozen
  broad beans
2 garlic cloves
3 tbsp extra-virgin olive oil,
  plus a little extra for drizzling

1 tbsp lemon juice
4 tbsp chopped fresh mint
salt and freshly ground black pepper
4 slices sourdough bread

1. Preheat the grill to high. Lay the pancetta on a grill rack resting over a tray. Grill for 4–5 minutes, until crisp. Set aside on the rack to cool.
2. Bring a large pan of lightly salted water to the boil. Add the beans and cook for 2–3 minutes if fresh, 4 minutes if frozen, until just tender. Drain well, refresh in cold water and drain again. Slip each bean out of its skin and into a large bowl.
3. Crush 1 garlic clove and put into a small bowl. Whisk together with the oil, lemon juice and some seasoning to make a dressing.
4. To serve, drizzle the dressing over the beans, add the mint and gently toss together. Toast the sourdough slices, then rub one side of each with the remaining garlic and drizzle with a little olive oil. Place one slice of bread on each plate and pile the beans on top. Top each with three pancetta slices.

Warm chicken & herb salad

Serves 2

3 chicken breasts, skins removed

2 tbsp olive oil

110g fine green beans, trimmed
and halved

20g fresh parsley, leaves only

20g fresh mint, leaves only

2 tbsp Dijon mustard

2 tbsp capers, drained

1 tbsp balsamic vinegar

100g mixed salad leaves

salt and freshly ground black pepper

1. Heat a griddle pan and boil the kettle. Cut the chicken into thickish strips and toss with 1 tsp of the oil and some seasoning.

2. Cook the chicken for 4 minutes on each side. Meanwhile, cook the beans in boiling water until tender, then drain.

3. Place the parsley, mint, mustard, capers, balsamic vinegar and the rest of the olive oil in a food processor and whiz together.

4. Toss the hot chicken strips and beans with the salad leaves and the dressing. Serve immediately.

This also works well using chunks of griddled salmon. For extra sustenance, serve with some warm, crusty bread.

Vietnamese salad

Illustrated on the following pages

Serves 4

2 large chicken breasts,
  skins removed
2 tbsp vegetable oil
4 tbsp peanuts, chopped
2 shallots, thinly sliced
1 head Chinese leaf
225g carrots, grated
6 spring onions, shredded
4 tbsp chopped fresh mint
25g bunch fresh coriander

For the dressing

2 red chillies, deseeded and chopped
3 garlic cloves, crushed
2 tbsp brown sugar
1 tbsp rice vinegar
juice of 1 large or 2 small limes
1 tbsp fish sauce
3 tbsp vegetable oil

1. Put the dressing ingredients in a bowl and whisk well. Set aside.

2. Brush the chicken breasts with 1 tbsp vegetable oil and cook on a hot griddle pan over a medium heat for about 5 minutes on each side, or until cooked through. Set aside to rest for 5 minutes, then cut into large strips.

3. For the salad, heat 1 tbsp vegetable oil in a small pan and fry the peanuts for 1–2 minutes, until golden. Remove with a slotted spoon and drain on kitchen paper. Set aside.

4. Add the shallots to the oil and fry for 3–4 minutes, until golden and crisp. Drain on kitchen paper and set aside.

5. Tear the Chinese leaf into pieces and put in a large bowl. Add the carrot, spring onions and mint. Toss well and spoon onto a large platter. Drizzle with the dressing and toss together. Scatter with the coriander, peanuts and shallots. Serve with the chicken strips.

All-day-breakfast salad

Serves 2

2 large, very fresh eggs
8 rashers smoked streaky bacon
1 baguettine or small French stick
12 cherry tomatoes, halved
150g mixed salad leaves,
　　including frisée
2 tbsp French dressing (see the
　　recipe on page 264)

1. Pour 2.5cm of boiling water into a small frying pan and bring back to a
very gentle simmer.
2. Gently break in the eggs, leave for 1 minute and then take off the heat.
Leave for 10 minutes while you prepare the rest of the salad.
3. Fry the bacon in a large non-stick frying pan until brown and crisp.
Leaving the fat in the pan, transfer the bacon onto some kitchen paper.
4. Slice the baguettine into six thin slices (you will have some left over) and
then cut each slice in half. Fry in the bacon fat until it is crisp on both sides.
5. Put the tomatoes into a large bowl with the salad leaves and dressing.
Chop the bacon and add to the bowl along with the warm croutons.
6. Toss together, divide between two plates and top with the poached eggs.
Serve with the extra bread on the side.

Tomato, fresh mint & lemon salad

Serves 6

700g tomatoes, using a mixture of
  Pomodorino, Sungold, midi,
  plum and Flavia tomatoes
110g sun-blushed tomatoes
large handful fresh mint,
  roughly shredded

zest of 1 lemon, juice of half
4 tbsp extra-virgin olive oil
½ tsp caster sugar
salt and freshly ground black pepper

1. Cut all the tomatoes into bite-sized pieces. Combine them in a bowl, mix in the lemon zest and set aside for 1 hour.

2. Meanwhile, make a dressing by whisking together the lemon juice, olive oil, seasoning and the sugar.

3. To serve, pour the dressing over the tomatoes, add the mint and mix well to combine.

Zesty herb & chilli crab salad with crostini

Serves 6

1 small baguette, thinly sliced
   diagonally into 18 pieces
75ml extra-virgin olive oil, plus
   extra for brushing
juice of ½ small lemon,
   plus wedges to serve
handful fresh chives, finely chopped
few sprigs fresh dill, finely chopped

3 tbsp finely chopped fresh parsley
   leaves
2 red chillies, deseeded, 1 finely
   chopped, 1 finely sliced
300g fresh white crabmeat, any
   shell discarded
150g mixed baby salad leaves
salt and freshly ground black pepper

Note: You will also need a 9cm ring mould or pastry cutter.

1. Preheat the grill to medium. For the crostini, place half the baguette slices on a large baking tray, season and brush all over with olive oil. Grill for about 1 minute each side, until golden. Set aside on a wire rack to cool and repeat with the remaining baguette.

2. In a bowl, mix together 75ml oil, the lemon juice, fresh herbs and chopped red chilli. Season to taste and set aside to infuse for 5 minutes.

3. Put the crabmeat into a large bowl and gradually mix in just over half of the herb mixture to bind. Season to taste.

4. Place the ring mould or pastry cutter on a plate. Press in some of the crab mix, then remove the ring. Repeat to make six starters.

5. To serve, top each with a small pile of salad leaves. Garnish with the sliced chilli, drizzle around the remaining herb oil and serve with the crostini and lemon wedges to squeeze over.

Classic Caesar salad

Serves 6

3 slices rye bread

1 garlic clove, crushed

3 tbsp olive oil

4 Little Gem lettuces, leaves
separated

50g fresh Parmesan

6 tbsp Caesar salad dressing
(see the recipe on page 274)

sea salt

1. First make the croutons for the salad. Preheat the oven to 200°C (fan 180°C), gas 6. Cut the crusts off the bread, then cut the bread into small pieces. Put into a roasting tin, sprinkle with the garlic, olive oil and a little sea salt, and mix together. Cook for 10 minutes. Leave to cool until needed.

2. Rinse the lettuce in a colander under cold running water. Shake dry.

3. Put a handful of the lettuce leaves in a bowl (tearing any large leaves) and sprinkle with the croutons.

4. Drag a vegetable peeler over the Parmesan and let a few shavings fall into the salad. Drizzle over some Caesar salad dressing.

To make this into a more substantial dish try adding small pieces of grilled bacon or strips of griddled chicken.

Tomato, peach & cumin salad

Serves 2
2 ripe peaches
4 large ripe tomatoes
½ tsp cumin seeds
2 garlic cloves, finely sliced
juice of ½ lemon

2 tbsp extra-virgin olive oil, plus
  extra to drizzle
8 fresh mint leaves, to garnish
salt and freshly ground black pepper
200g Feta or goats' cheese, to serve

1. Skin the peaches and tomatoes in the same way. Score the stalk ends with an 'X'. Plunge into boiling water for 20 seconds, then transfer to cold water. As soon as they are cool enough to handle, peel away the skins. Stone the peaches, deseed the tomatoes and cut both into wedges. Transfer to a bowl.
2. Heat a frying pan or wok. Dry-fry the cumin seeds for about 30 seconds, until they start to smell roasted – you cannot mistake the aroma. Roughly crush them in a pestle and mortar, then add to the peaches and tomatoes with the garlic.
3. Whisk the lemon juice and olive oil with some salt and pepper into a salad dressing. Toss through the salad. Allow the salad to sit for up to an hour.
4. To serve, garnish with mint leaves and some crumbled Feta or goats' cheese that has been drizzled with olive oil.

Once you've tried this, you'll be hooked. It also makes a great accompaniment to grilled fish, shellfish and meat dishes.

Coriander & coconut crab salad

Serves 2

1 avocado, peeled and stoned
1 little gem lettuce, shredded
½ cucumber, peeled and diced
2 tbsp lemon juice
25g bunch fresh coriander,
  stalks removed

3 tbsp coconut milk
3 tbsp soured cream
grated zest of 1 lemon
few shakes of Tabasco
1 dressed crab
salt and freshly ground black pepper
thick slices of buttered soda bread

1. Chop the avocado into small chunks and toss with the lettuce, cucumber and 1 tbsp of the lemon juice in a bowl. Divide between two bowls.
2. Whiz the coriander in a processor until finely chopped. Add the coconut milk, soured cream, remaining lemon juice, lemon zest and Tabasco. Season and whiz together.
3. Toss the dressing with the crab and add to the bowls. Serve with some buttered soda bread.

If you can't source a fresh dressed crab then use a 170g can of crabmeat, drained, instead.

Goats' cheese & beetroot salad

Serves 6

4 bunches baby red beetroot with
   tops, about 300g (use half yellow
   beetroot if you can find some)
1 tbsp red-wine vinegar
1 tbsp cider vinegar
2 good pinches of sugar
2 sprigs fresh thyme
2 fresh bay leaves
2 garlic cloves, halved
50g butter
1 sprig fresh rosemary
50g walnut pieces, plus a few extra

200g goats' cheese, diced
1 baby white chicory, leaves
   separated
1 baby red chicory, leaves separated
120g wild rocket leaves
salt and freshly ground black pepper

For the vinaigrette
3 tbsp extra-virgin olive oil
1 tbsp walnut oil
1 tbsp cider vinegar
salt and freshly ground black pepper

1. If you've managed to source yellow beetroot, line two saucepans with foil.
Put the red beetroot, its tops and the wine vinegar in one, and the yellow
beetroot, its tops and the cider vinegar in the other. Add a pinch of sugar,
a thyme sprig, a bay leaf and two garlic halves to each. If you only have
red beetroot, double up on the ingredients and use one slightly larger pan.
Gather up the foil to form a loose parcel and seal in the ingredients.
2. Pour water to about one-third of the way up the side of each parcel. Cover,
bring to the boil, reduce and simmer for 20–30 minutes, until just tender.
3. Drain the parcels, saving 1 tbsp of liquid from the red beetroot parcel. When
cool enough to handle, peel the beetroot with a small knife. Cut into wedges.
4. Heat the butter gently in a small pan until it reaches the beurre noisette
stage (when it turns a nutty brown colour). Add the rosemary sprig and
50g walnut pieces. Cook gently for 1–2 minutes, coating the nuts in the butter.
Discard the rosemary, drain off the butter and set the nuts aside. Make the
dressing: whisk the oils, vinegar and reserved liquid. Season and set aside.
5. In a bowl, mix the beetroot with a little dressing. Divide between serving
plates and scatter over the cheese. Put the chicory and rocket into a bowl
and toss with some dressing. Divide between each plate. Season with black
pepper and scatter with the walnuts. Drizzle the rest of the dressing over the
cheese. To serve, finely grate the extra walnuts over the salads.

Crab, avocado & crispy bacon salad

Serves 2

135g mixed salad of watercress,
   rocket and spinach
1 ripe avocado, stoned, peeled
   and sliced
30g toasted pine nuts

40g cooked crispy bacon
100g fresh white crabmeat
3 tbsp olive oil
1 tbsp lemon juice
salt and freshly ground black pepper

1. Divide the salad between two large serving plates. Dot over the avocado, pine nuts and broken up pieces of crispy bacon. Top with the crabmeat.
2. In a small bowl, whisk together the olive oil and lemon juice. Season to taste and drizzle over the salad to serve.

If you can't source fresh crabmeat then use a 170g can of crabmeat, drained, instead.

Sticky spare ribs & crunchy slaw

Serves 6

1.5kg pork spare ribs

6 tbsp dark soy sauce

3 tbsp kecap manis

4 tbsp honey

60g fresh ginger, sliced into
thick rounds

4 spring onions

3 tbsp Chinese rice wine or
sherry vinegar

For the crunchy slaw

6 spring onions, thinly sliced

1 large carrot, cut into short,
thin strips

1 small cucumber, cut into short,
thin strips

2 tbsp mayonnaise (see the recipe
on page 278)

3 tbsp olive oil

juice of 1 lime, plus extra lime
wedges, to serve

salt and freshly ground black pepper

1. Put the spare ribs in a large non-stick roasting tin. Mix the soy sauce, kecap manis and honey in a bowl and pour over the ribs. Add the ginger, whole spring onions and rice wine.

2. Put the tin on the hob, pour over 1 litre of water and bring to the boil. Cover with foil and simmer over a medium heat for 45 minutes, turning regularly to ensure the ribs cook evenly.

3. Put all the slaw ingredients in a serving bowl, season, and toss well.

4. Remove and discard the ginger and spring onions from the rib mixture. Increase the heat to high and cook, uncovered, for a further 30–40 minutes, until the sauce is thick and syrupy. Once cooked, the ribs should be evenly coated with a dark glaze and the meat should be very tender.

5. To serve, pile the ribs and pan juices on a platter, put the bowl of slaw alongside and serve with the lime wedges to squeeze over.

The crunchy slaw makes a lovely contrast to these finger-licking sticky ribs. Kecap manis is an Indonesian sweet soy sauce.

Squid, lemon & caper salad

Serves 4

600g squid, cleaned, gutted and cut into rings (ask your fishmonger to do this)

juice of 3 unwaxed lemons, with their leaves if possible, plus extra lemon wedges to serve

2 tbsp capers, soaked and rinsed if packed in salt

3 garlic cloves, finely sliced

5 whole black peppercorns

40g pitted Kalamata, halved, or whole small black olives

100ml extra-virgin olive oil

salt

1. Put a generous handful of salt into a large pan of water and bring to a rolling boil. Blanch the squid in the pan for no more than 30 seconds, then drain. Alternatively, sear it on a ridged griddle or cast-iron frying pan for about 30 seconds on either side.

2. Using a potato peeler or fruit knife, peel four or five strips of lemon zest and put them in a mixing bowl. If the lemons have leaves, destalk and shred two of them to add to the zest. (You could use bay leaves instead.)

3. Add the capers to the bowl with the lemon juice, garlic, peppercorns, olives and oil. Mix thoroughly, then stir in the squid while still warm. Cover and marinate in the fridge, ideally overnight.

4. Serve with lemon wedges. It shouldn't need salt but check to make sure.

This is actually best made a day ahead, so is good for entertaining. It is great served with thin slices of fennel or chicory, on toast or tossed with some warm new potatoes.

Warm salad of pear, scallop & chorizo

Serves 4

100g chorizo, skinned and thinly
sliced

12 fresh scallops, shucked and
washed but whole with orange
roe left on

2 medium, firm pears, cored and
thinly sliced

1 tbsp sherry vinegar

75g bunch of watercress,
washed and destalked

1 tbsp olive oil

salt

1. Make sure you have everything prepared before you start cooking.
Gently heat a non-stick frying pan. When hot, add the chorizo and dry-fry
until just beginning to brown – it will release its own oil after 30 seconds
or so. Remove with a slotted spoon and set aside on kitchen paper.

2. Add the scallops to the pan and sear in the chorizo oil for about 1 minute
each side. Remove and set aside with the chorizo.

3. Finally, add the pear slices and fry quite briskly to caramelise a little.
Once you have turned them, add the vinegar and swirl the pears around in
it for a few seconds, then tip it all into a bowl.

4. Add the scallops, chorizo, watercress and oil. Season with salt (not pepper
in case the chorizo has a kick of its own). Serve immediately.

Be demanding when you shop for this recipe.
You want a good chorizo (the thinner, dryer
kind is best); firm pears (the harder the
better); and look for diver-caught scallops.

Chicory & apple salad

Serves 4

2 heads of chicory

2 Golden Delicious apples, quartered,
  cored and thinly sliced

100g Roquefort cheese

50g toasted walnuts

1 tbsp Dijon mustard

2 tbsp walnut oil

2 tbsp olive oil

salt and freshly ground pepper

1. Cut the chicory heads in half, take off the outside leaves, then quarter the inside bulb. Arrange the leaves and bulbs on serving plates with the apples over the top.

2. Crumble the cheese over the leaves, along with the walnuts.

3. Make a quick dressing by whisking together the mustard and both oils in a small bowl. Season with a little salt and some freshly ground black pepper. Drizzle over the salad to serve.

Golden Delicious apples don't discolour as quickly as other varieties when they are cut, making them a good choice to use in salads.

salads
beef, pork & lamb

Tagliata (seared steak & rocket salad)

Serves 2

400g small baby new potatoes

2 x 150g beef steaks, such as rib-eye or sirloin, about 2cm thick

1 tsp Dijon mustard

1 tbsp balsamic vinegar

1 tbsp capers

3 tbsp extra-virgin olive oil

1 tbsp finely chopped fresh tarragon

50g rocket leaves

salt and freshly ground black pepper

1. Boil the potatoes until tender, then drain. Allow to cool slightly.

2. Meanwhile, sear the steaks in a hot, dry frying pan for about 2 minutes each side (this will leave them rare, so if you prefer your meat medium-rare, make it 3 minutes each side). Rest the steaks once they are cooked.

3. Make the salad. Cut the still-warm potatoes in half (or break them up with your hands) and toss with the mustard, vinegar, capers, 2 tbsp extra-virgin olive oil and the tarragon.

4. Slice the steak as thinly as you can and toss it into the salad with the rocket. Season with salt, pepper and the remaining oil.

This is an Anglicised version of an Italian dish of rare, sliced steak dressed with balsamic vinegar. Hunt down some good beef, properly aged balsamic vinegar and early Jersey Royal potatoes to make this really special.

Griddled beef salad with mushrooms

Serves 2

1 tbsp capers, drained

2 cloves garlic, peeled and roughly chopped

2 tsp Dijon mustard

20g fresh flat-leaf parsley

20g fresh basil

6 tbsp olive oil

250g chestnut mushrooms

2 x 225g sirloin steaks

150g mixed herb salad

salt and freshly ground black pepper

crusty bread, to serve

1. Put the capers, garlic, mustard, parsley, basil, 5 tbsp of olive oil and some black pepper in a small food processor; whiz to make a coarse purée. Thickly slice the mushrooms.

2. Heat a large griddle pan over a high heat. Brush both sides of the steaks with some of the remaining oil and season with pepper. Cook for 1–2 minutes on each side (they will be pink inside), pressing them on to the pan with a fish slice. Remove to a plate.

3. Add the mushrooms to the griddle along with the rest of the oil, if needed, and cook for 4 minutes, tossing now and then.

4. Slice the beef and sprinkle with sea salt. Toss the beef with its juices, the mushrooms, salad leaves and dressing together in a large bowl and serve with warm, crusty bread.

Seared steak, mango & radish salad

Serves 2

2 x 150g sirloin steaks
1 tbsp vegetable oil
150g radishes
1 ripe mango
130g herb leaf salad
French dressing for drizzling
   (see the recipe on page 264)
salt and freshly ground black pepper

1. Trim and discard the fat from the sirloin steaks, then season and cut into thin strips.
2. Heat the vegetable oil in a wok or large frying pan over a high heat. Add the beef, in batches, and stir-fry for a few minutes until the meat is browned. Set aside on a plate lined with kitchen paper to cool slightly.
3. Slice the radishes; peel, stone and slice the mango. Put both into a large bowl and mix gently together.
4. Add the beef and the salad leaves. Season, drizzle with French dressing and gently toss to serve.

Hot Thai beef salad

Serves 2

1 garlic clove, chopped
1½ tsp brown sugar
1 tbsp lime juice
2 tbsp light soy sauce
½ cucumber
handful of beansprouts

1 red chilli, deseeded and finely
  sliced
large handful of mint leaves
1 Little Gem lettuce
2 x 150g sirloin or rump steaks
salt and freshly ground black pepper

1. First make the dressing. Chop the garlic clove and, in a bowl, whisk with
the brown sugar, lime juice and soy sauce. Set aside.
2. Halve and deseed the cucumber, cut into sticks and put into a bowl.
Deseed and finely slice the chilli and add to the bowl with the beansprouts,
mint leaves and the torn-up leaves of the lettuce. Toss well and divide
between two plates.
3. Heat a griddle, frying pan or grill. Season the steaks and cook them
for 2–5 minutes on each side, depending on how well done you like them.
4. Place the steaks on a board and cut into slices. Divide between the plates
and drizzle with the dressing.

Griddled steak with potatoes & peppers

Serves 2

315g new potatoes

2 x 200g sirloin steaks, trimmed

150g mixed pepper antipasto,
   drained and chopped, the oil
   marinade reserved

25g wild rocket leaves

1 tbsp small capers, rinsed and
   drained

salt and freshly ground black pepper

1. Bring a pan of salted water to the boil. Cook the potatoes for 15 minutes until tender.

2. Meanwhile, brush the steaks with 2 tbsp of the marinade from the peppers. Season with black pepper and leave to one side for 5 minutes.

3. Heat a griddle pan until very hot, then fry the steaks for 3 minutes on each side, remove to a board and leave to rest for 5 minutes.

4. Drain the potatoes and, when cool enough to handle, thickly slice them into a bowl. Add the rocket, capers, peppers and 2 tbsp of the pepper marinade. Season and toss together.

5. Season the steaks with a little salt, slice them in half and serve on top of the salad. Drizzle with any extra juices.

Warm new potato & smoked sausage salad

Illustrated on the following pages

Serves 4
600g anya or baby new potatoes
2 x 225g packs smoked pork
    sausage or frankfurter
1 small red onion, peeled, halved and
    thinly sliced into half moons
20g fresh dill, fronds chopped
4 large handfuls rocket leaves
salt

For the dressing
1½ tbsp Dijon mustard
3 tbsp red-wine vinegar
2 tsp caster sugar
2 tbsp small capers
6 tbsp extra-virgin olive oil
salt and freshly ground black pepper

1. Cook the new potatoes for 10–15 minutes in boiling salted water until easily pierced with a knife.
2. Meanwhile, bring another pan of water to the boil and add the smoked sausage. Cook for 15 minutes, then cut into 1cm slices.
3. Place the dressing ingredients and some salt and pepper in a lidded jar. Shake well, then set aside.
4. Drain the potatoes and let them cool slightly before slicing. Place them in a medium bowl with the onion, dill and sausage.
5. Pour the dressing over and gently mix. Divide between four plates with a handful of rocket and serve.

Smoked pork sausage is surprisingly versatile. It keeps well in the fridge and is ideal for soups, sandwiches and salads.

Warm mozzarella, bacon & nectarine

Serves 4
250g diced bacon
4 tbsp olive oil
150g mozzarella
2 nectarines

2 tbsp sherry vinegar
2 tsp mustard
200g rocket salad
8 fresh mint leaves
salt and freshly ground black pepper

1. Fry the bacon in 1 tbsp olive oil until crispy. Drain on kitchen paper.
2. Drain the mozzarella and tear into pieces. Halve the nectarines, stone them, and slice each half into four.
3. In a small pan, whisk together the sherry vinegar, 3 tbsp olive oil and the mustard. Warm through.
4. Put the rocket salad in a large bowl and add the bacon and nectarines. Tear the mint leaves over the top.
5. Toss with the warm dressing, some seasoning and the mozzarella. Serve immediately.

Warm potato salad with Parma ham

Serves 6

2 large red peppers
600g Jersey Royal new potatoes, scrubbed
4 tsp extra-virgin olive oil, plus extra for drizzling
1 tbsp chopped fresh flat-leaf parsley
12 thin slices Parma ham
50g baby salad leaves
½ tsp white-wine vinegar

1. Preheat the oven to 220°C (fan 200°C), gas 7. Roast the whole peppers for 20–25 minutes, until lightly charred. Seal in a plastic bag and cool. Remove and discard the stalks, seeds and skin. Cut into strips.
2. Cook the potatoes in plenty of boiling, salted water for 10–12 minutes or until tender. Drain. When cool enough to handle, thickly slice into a large bowl. Fold in the oil and parsley.
3. To serve, ruffle two slices of Parma ham onto each plate, then pile over some of the salad leaves. Stir the vinegar into the potatoes, season, and arrange on top of the salad along with the red pepper strips. Drizzle over a little more oil and serve at once.

To get ahead you can prepare the peppers the day before and chill overnight. Bring them back up to room temperature before using.

BLT salad

Illustrated on the following pages

Serves 4
½ ciabatta
olive oil, for drizzling
10–12 rashers dry-cure smoked
  streaky bacon
85g wild rocket leaves
120g baby spinach leaves
16 cherry tomatoes, halved
salt and freshly ground black pepper

For the dressing
4 tbsp good mayonnaise
  (see the recipe on page 278)
1 small clove garlic, peeled and
  crushed
2 tsp grainy mustard
1 tbsp sherry vinegar
4 tbsp olive oil

1. Cut the bread into cubes, toss them in a little olive oil with some
seasoning, and tip into a frying pan. Toast over a low heat for 4–5 minutes.
Leave to cool.
2. Mix the dressing ingredients together in a bowl with 1 tbsp of cold water.
Grill the bacon under a hot grill on both sides until really crispy, then halve
widthways.
3. Toss the leaves in a bowl with the dressing. Divide between four bowls,
layering with the tomatoes, croûtons and bacon as you go, and serve.

Sicilian sausages with lentils

Serves 2–3

6 Sicilian-style sausages

1 small aubergine, sliced lengthways into 5mm slices

1 large courgette, sliced lengthways into 5mm slices

4 tbsp olive oil

125g ready-roasted red peppers, drained and sliced

410g can green lentils in water, drained and rinsed

1½ tbsp sherry vinegar

1½ tbsp chopped fresh mint

½ small red onion, peeled and thinly sliced

salt and freshly ground black pepper

1. Preheat the grill to high and cook the sausages on a rack for 15 minutes, turning now and then so that they cook evenly.

2. Meanwhile heat a griddle pan. Brush the aubergine and courgette slices with oil and griddle until marked on both sides. Set aside.

3. In a saucepan, combine the peppers with the lentils, vinegar and 2 tbsp of the oil. Warm over a low heat.

4. Cut the aubergine and courgette slices into smaller pieces and add to the lentils with the mint, the red onion and seasoning. Heat for 1 minute and serve with the sausages.

Sicilian sausages are aromatic and full of flavour. They are spiced with fennel, red wine, fresh garlic and herbs. If you can't find them use good quality pork sausages instead.

Paprika-spiced pork

Serves 4

3 small lemons

500g pork fillet (tenderloin), trimmed of all fat and cut into 32 small pieces

4 garlic cloves, crushed

1 tsp dried oregano

1 tsp each ground cumin, coriander and turmeric

2 tsp paprika

4 tbsp Greek yogurt

16 fresh bay leaves

16 pickled whole red chillies (optional)

3 red onions, thickly sliced

3 beef tomatoes, thickly sliced

1 tbsp olive oil

balsamic vinegar, for drizzling

large handful fresh flat-leaf parsley, roughly torn

Note: You will also need 8 metal skewers.

1. Finely grate the zest from 1 lemon and squeeze the juice. Put both into a bowl with the pork, garlic, oregano, ground spices and yogurt. Mix well, cover and set aside to marinate for at least 20 minutes (or up to 2 hours, if you have time).

2. Preheat the grill to hot. Cut each of the remaining lemons into eight wedges. Thread four pieces of pork, two wedges of lemon, two bay leaves and two chillies, if using, alternately on each skewer. Arrange on a large foil-lined grill tray and grill for 15 minutes, turning, until the pork is cooked through and lightly charred.

3. Meanwhile, preheat the oven to 180°C (fan 160°C), gas 4 and heat a large griddle pan until smoking. Brush the onions and tomatoes with the oil and season well. Chargrill the onions on the griddle for 5 minutes, turn them over and cook for a further 2 minutes. Transfer to a baking dish and keep hot in the oven while you cook the tomatoes. Add the tomatoes to the griddle pan and chargrill for 2–3 minutes, without turning.

4. Pile the tomatoes onto serving plates with the onions and sprinkle with some balsamic vinegar and flat-leaf parsley. Arrange the spiced pork skewers on top to serve.

Niçoise salad of bacon & cheesy croûtons

Serves 4

200g ciabatta loaf, torn into pieces
3 tbsp extra-virgin olive oil
25g fresh Parmesan, grated
6 rashers streaky bacon, chopped
100g trimmed fine green beans
1 cos lettuce, cut into bite-sized
  pieces

4 ripe tomatoes, cut into wedges
50g pitted black olives
4 eggs, hard-boiled
salt and freshly ground black pepper
French dressing, to serve (see the
  recipe on page 264)

1. Preheat oven to 220°C (fan 200°C), gas 7. Put the ciabatta pieces in a roasting tin, add the oil and turn to coat. Scatter over the cheese, season with pepper and mix. Stir in the chopped bacon. Cook for 15 minutes, turning halfway, until golden. Drain on kitchen paper.

2. Meanwhile, add the green beans to a small saucepan of boiling water. Cook for 2 minutes, then drain and plunge into cold water to cool. Drain well and set aside.

3. Divide the lettuce between four plates. Top with the green beans, tomato wedges, olives, the cheesy ciabatta croûtons and the bacon. Season. Peel and cut the eggs into wedges and scatter over the salad. Drizzle with French dressing to serve.

Make the croûtons the day before, put in an airtight container and store in a cool place.

Apple & pork salad with cider dressing

Serves 2

2 thick slices of bread
5 tbsp olive oil
200g pork tenderloin fillet
1 Cox's apple
1 tbsp cider vinegar
130g of salad leaves
salt and freshly ground black pepper

1. Cut off and discard the crusts from the bread. Cut the bread into cubes. Heat 3 tbsp olive oil in a frying pan and cook the bread for 4–5 minutes, tossing regularly. Drain on kitchen paper and set aside.
2. Trim any fat from the pork fillet and cut into six thick slices. Flatten each piece slightly.
3. Wipe out the frying pan with kitchen paper. Heat 1 tbsp olive oil in the pan and fry the pork for 5–6 minutes, turning once. Remove from the pan and set aside.
4. Cut the apple into twelve wedges and fry in the same pan for 1–2 minutes, turning once, until dark golden. Remove and set aside. Add the cider vinegar and 1 tbsp olive oil and sizzle briefly. Season well.
5. Toss the salad leaves with the homemade croutons and apple wedges and divide between two plates. Top with the pork and drizzle with the dressing.

Ham with peach & couscous

Illustrated on the previous pages

Serves 2

75g couscous

2.5cm piece fresh ginger,
   finely grated

2 ripe peaches

1 cucumber

4 spring onions, sliced

3 tbsp chopped fresh mint

2–3 slices of cooked ham

salt and freshly ground black pepper

1. Put the couscous into a bowl with the ginger. Pour over 75ml boiling water and set aside for 5 minutes.

2. Meanwhile, stone and cut the peaches into thin wedges and place in a bowl.

3. Cut the cucumber in half lengthways and scoop out and discard the seeds. Cut into dice and mix with the peaches.

4. Add the spring onions to the bowl with the fresh mint.

5. Loosen up the couscous and stir in the peach mixture just before serving. Check the seasoning. Divide the couscous salad between two plates, then add two or three slices of cooked ham to serve.

Minted lamb kebabs with beans & rocket

Serves 6
3 tbsp mint sauce
juice of 1 small lemon, plus wedges
to serve
3 tbsp olive oil
4 lamb steaks, cubed
2 small red onions, 1 cubed;
1 finely sliced

1 red pepper, deseeded and cut into
squares
250g halloumi cheese, cubed
2 x 410g cans mixed pulses, drained
and rinsed
125g rocket leaves
salt and freshly ground black pepper

Note: You will also need 12 bamboo skewers.

1. Soak the bamboo skewers in water for 30 minutes to stop them from
burning during cooking. Preheat the grill to high.
2. Meanwhile, in a bowl, mix the mint sauce, half the lemon juice and 1 tbsp
olive oil. Add the lamb, cubed onion, red pepper and halloumi. Season and
mix to coat. Cover and leave for 15 minutes, or chill overnight.
3. Put the pulses in a serving bowl with the sliced onion. Add the remaining
lemon juice and oil, season and mix. Set aside, covered.
4. Thread the lamb, onion, pepper and halloumi onto the skewers, being
gentle with the halloumi to avoid breaking it. Cook under the hot grill on a
baking sheet lined with foil, for 10 minutes, turning halfway, until they are
cooked through and lightly charred. Divide between serving plates. Stir the
rocket through the pulses and serve with the kebabs and lemon wedges.

Halloumi is a traditional, salty cheese from
Cyprus. It's texture makes it ideal for grilling
and griddle-frying.

Warm Sunday roast salad

Serves 6
2–2.5kg leg of lamb
4 garlic cloves, cut into slivers
few sprigs fresh rosemary
450g baby new potatoes
175ml olive oil
200g French green beans

4 tbsp red-wine vinegar
generous pinch of sugar
3 tbsp freshly chopped mint
600g cherry tomatoes, halved
350g baby spinach leaves, rocket or
  watercress, or a mixture
salt and freshly ground black pepper

1. Preheat the oven to 220°C (fan 200°C), gas 7. With the tip of a small, sharp knife make slits all over the lamb. Insert a sliver of garlic and a sprig of rosemary into each slit.

2. Weigh the lamb and calculate the cooking time. Cook for 20 minutes, then reduce the oven temperature to 190°C (fan 170°C), gas 5 and roast for a further 20 minutes per 450g. This will give a slightly pink lamb. Add an extra 20 minutes if you like it medium.

3. Meanwhile, cook the potatoes in boiling, salted water for 10–15 minutes, until tender. Drain and spill into a roasting tin, drizzle with 2 tbsp of oil and season. Roast for 30 minutes before the lamb is done.

4. Cook the beans in boiling, salted water, drain and refresh under cold running water. Drain again and set aside.

5. Make the dressing: whisk together the remaining oil, vinegar, sugar, mint and plenty of seasoning.

6. Take the lamb and potatoes out of the oven. Leave the lamb to rest for about 15 minutes and let the potatoes cool (they both only need to be just warm when served).

7. Slice the lamb and put on to a plate. Put the tomatoes, salad leaves, green beans and warm potatoes into a large bowl and toss well. Drizzle with enough dressing to coat and toss again. Add the lamb to serve. Put the rest of the dressing into a jug for everyone to help themselves.

Lamb & aubergine with pomegranate

Serves 4

For the marinade/dressing
6 tbsp pomegranate molasses
juice of ½ lemon
2 cloves garlic, peeled and crushed
6 tbsp extra-virgin olive oil
1 tsp caster sugar
salt and freshly ground black pepper

For the salad
600g lamb leg steaks
2 aubergines, cut into 2cm slices

2 tsp ground cinnamon
200g fine green beans, trimmed
3 tbsp roughly chopped flat-leaf
  parsley
1 small red onion, peeled and
  chopped
salt and freshly ground black pepper

To serve
4 tbsp Greek yogurt
4 pitta breads or flatbreads

1. Combine the marinade/dressing ingredients with some salt and pepper in a screw-top jar. Shake well and set aside.

2. Put the lamb steaks and aubergine slices into a large non-metallic dish. Season and sprinkle with the cinnamon. Pour a third of the marinade over both and mix together until thoroughly combined. Cover and marinate in the fridge for 3–4 hours. Remove from the fridge 45 minutes before cooking.

3. Blanch the green beans in boiling salted water for 3–4 minutes or until tender, then drain in a colander and rinse in cold water.

4. Heat the griddle pan until hot. Griddle the lamb steaks for 2–3 minutes on each side (this will give you pink lamb). Remove and leave the meat to rest for 5 minutes on a board.

5. While the lamb rests, griddle the aubergine in batches for 2–3 minutes on each side or until softened (discard any marinade on the aubergine). Arrange the aubergine in a dish. Toast the pitta breads lightly under the grill.

6. Slice the lamb and arrange over the aubergine. Sprinkle with the parsley, red onion and green beans then pour the remaining dressing over before serving with a bowl of Greek yogurt and the toasted pitta breads.

salads
fish &
shellfish

Tuna, fennel & white bean salad

Serves 4

1 small head fennel
1 medium red onion, halved
2 x 400g cans cannellini beans,
  drained and rinsed
2 tbsp extra-virgin olive oil

3 tbsp lemon juice
3 tbsp chopped fresh flat-leaf parsley
2 x 200g cans tuna steak in spring
  water, drained
60g black olives, pitted if you prefer
salt and freshly ground black pepper

1. Trim the base and tops off the fennel and save the fennel fronds to use
as a garnish. Core, then slice the head across as thinly as you can into
horseshoe-shaped slices – use a mandolin if you have one. Slice the onion
in the same way.

2. Put the fennel and onion into a large bowl with the beans, olive oil, lemon
juice, parsley and some seasoning to taste. Stir together well and leave for
about 5 minutes for the fennel to soften slightly.

3. Break the drained tuna into large flakes and gently stir into the bean and
fennel salad.

4. Spoon the salad into the centre of four plates and scatter with the black
olives. Garnish with the fennel fronds.

Seared tuna with bean & olive salad

Serves 3

410g can cannellini beans,
  drained and rinsed
1 small red onion, finely sliced
2 celery sticks, finely sliced
French dressing, for drizzling
  (see the recipe on page 264)

50g rocket leaves
3 fresh tuna steaks
2 tbsps olive oil
24 black olives
salt and freshly ground black pepper

1. Put the cannellini beans into a bowl. Add the red onion and the celery. Drizzle with a little French dressing and season well.
2. Divide the rocket between three serving plates and spoon the bean mix over the leaves.
3. Heat a griddle. Brush the tuna steaks with olive oil and fry on the griddle for 2–3 minutes each side.
4. Serve a tuna steak with each salad and scatter with the black olives.

You could replace the fresh tuna with a large can of tuna in oil, drained.

Tuna & pesto pasta salad

Serves 4

225g pasta shapes of your choice

2 tsp ready-made green pesto

185g can tuna steak in olive oil, drained

⅓ cucumber, chopped into chunky pieces

100g cherry tomatoes, halved

4 tbsp French dressing (see the recipe on page 264)

salt and freshly ground black pepper

1. Boil the pasta in a large saucepan of salted water, until just cooked and still firm to the bite. Drain well and transfer the pasta to a large serving bowl. Leave to cool slightly.

2. Stir in the pesto. Roughly flake the tuna and stir into the pasta, with the chopped cucumber and tomatoes. Season and add the French dressing. Stir well before serving.

This is perfect as a packed lunch, and it's healthy, too. Try it with other salad vegetables like sliced pepper, capers or a few pitted olives.

Tuna & cannellini bean salad

Serves 4

2 x 200g cans tuna in olive oil

250g cherry tomatoes, roughly
   chopped

12 spring onions, roughly chopped

2 x 410g cans cannellini beans,
   drained

2 tbsp capers, rinsed

100g rocket leaves

2 tbsp balsamic vinegar

8 tbsp extra-virgin olive oil

salt and freshly ground black pepper

1. Drain the tuna, flake into bite-sized pieces and place in a salad bowl.

2. Add the cherry tomatoes and spring onions to the tuna, along with the cannellini beans and capers.

3. Place the remaining ingredients in the bowl of a food processor and whiz until the rocket is finely chopped and the dressing is combined. Season, mix into the salad and serve.

The flavours in this salad improve if you make it a little in advance. Cover and set aside for about 45 minutes before serving. Look out for albacore tuna in extra-virgin olive oil to use in this recipe.

Chargrilled pesto tuna with potato salad

Serves 4

475g new potatoes
6 tbsp aïoli (see the recipe on
    page 282)
2 tbsp chopped fresh basil

3 tbsp sun-dried tomato pesto,
    plus a little more to serve
1 tbsp olive oil
4 x 175g tuna steaks
salt and freshly ground black pepper

1. Put the new potatoes in a pan of salted water and bring to the boil. Cover and simmer for 20 minutes, until tender. Drain and rinse under cold water until they are cold.

2. Roughly chop the potatoes and put into a bowl with the aïoli and chopped basil. Season to taste and gently mix together.

3. Meanwhile, mix the sun-dried tomato pesto with the olive oil and brush over the tuna steaks.

4. Heat a griddle pan. When very hot, add the tuna and sear for 2–3 minutes on each side, until cooked but still a little pink in the middle.

5. Divide between four plates and drizzle with a little extra pesto. Serve with the potato salad and cooked green beans.

Tuna salad with beans, capers & new potatoes

Serves 2
2 tuna steaks
2 tbsp olive oil
2 tsp soy sauce
juice of ½ lemon

1 tbsp capers, rinsed and drained
handful fresh chives, chopped
350g small new potatoes
100g fine green beans
salt and freshly ground black pepper

1. Boil the kettle. Meanwhile, marinate the tuna in ½ tbsp of the oil, the soy sauce, some black pepper and 1 tbsp of the lemon juice.

2. Put the remaining oil and lemon juice, the capers, chives and some salt and pepper into a large bowl, mix together and set aside.

3. Pour boiling water from the kettle into a pan, add the potatoes and some salt and boil for 15 minutes, adding the beans for the final 4 minutes.

4. When the vegetables are nearly ready, heat a griddle pan until very hot then cook the tuna steaks for 1 minute on each side (if they are very thick or if you prefer them well-done, they will need a little longer). Rest on a plate while you drain the vegetables.

5. Toss the vegetables with the dressing and serve with the tuna.

Prawn, watercress & spinach salad

Illustrated on the following pages

Serves 4

400g cooked king prawns with tails
85g watercress, stalks removed
150g sugar snaps, halved
   lengthways
225g baby spinach leaves
3 spring onions
1 large firm, ripe mango
1 large lime
1½ tbsp fresh coriander, leaves only

For the dressing

3 tbsps Thai fish sauce
juice of 1 lime
1 tbsp caster sugar
1 medium red chilli, deseeded and
   finely chopped
1 thumbnail-sized piece ginger,
   peeled and finely grated
1 large clove garlic, peeled and
   finely chopped
3 tbsps groundnut or vegetable oil

1. Put the prawns in a large bowl, leaving all or a few of the tails on. Add the watercress and sugar snaps to the bowl together with the spinach leaves.
2. Trim the spring onions, halve them lengthways, then slice them on the diagonal into small pieces and add them to the bowl.
3. Slice the 'cheeks' off either side of the mango stone, peel them, and slice the flesh into long thin slivers. Remove the flesh from the stone and slice that, too. Add the mango slices to the bowl.
4. Pare the skin and pith from the lime, then chop the flesh into small pieces and put in the bowl, followed by the coriander leaves.
5. In a jug, whisk together all the dressing ingredients. To serve, toss the salad ingredients together with the dressing and serve immediately.

This dish is lightly spiced, but if you want the dressing to have a real kick, leave the seeds in the chilli.

Prawn, orange & fennel salad

Serves 4

1 fennel bulb, sliced very finely,
   reserve the fronds
125g mixed salad leaves
16 large prawns, peeled and cooked
2 oranges
9 tbsp extra-virgin olive oil
1 chilli, deseeded and finely chopped
salt and freshly ground black pepper

1. Divide the sliced fennel between four plates. Add a good handful of the mixed salad leaves to each and top with four prawns.
2. Segment the oranges and let the segments and juice fall into a bowl. Divide the segments between the plates.
3. Take 3 tbsps of the orange juice and whisk with the extra-virgin olive oil, the chilli and chopped fennel fronds. Season well and drizzle the dressing over each plate to serve.

The chilli and fennel add a more complex flavour to this fresh, light meal.

Strawberry & langoustine salad

Serves 4

50g pine nuts

3 generous slices fresh pineapple

12 cooked langoustines

2 Little Gem lettuces, leaves
   separated

450g strawberries, washed, hulled
   and quartered

For the dressing

2 tbsp red-wine vinegar

3 tbsp extra-virgin olive oil

1 tsp clear honey

1 tsp Dijon mustard

½ tsp salt

1. Toss the pine nuts in a large dry pan over a medium heat for 4–5 minutes, until golden brown. Set aside to cool completely.

2. Meanwhile, make the dressing by whisking all the ingredients together. Set aside.

3. Slice the pineapple into segments of a similar size to the strawberries.

4. Peel the langoustines, reserving a couple of whole ones to garnish.

5. Toss the lettuce leaves and fruit with the dressing and arrange in a bowl. Put the peeled langoustines on top and arrange the langoustines still in the shell on the side. Sprinkle with the pine nuts to serve.

Langoustines are increasingly known as Dublin Bay prawns. You could use prawns instead of langoustines.

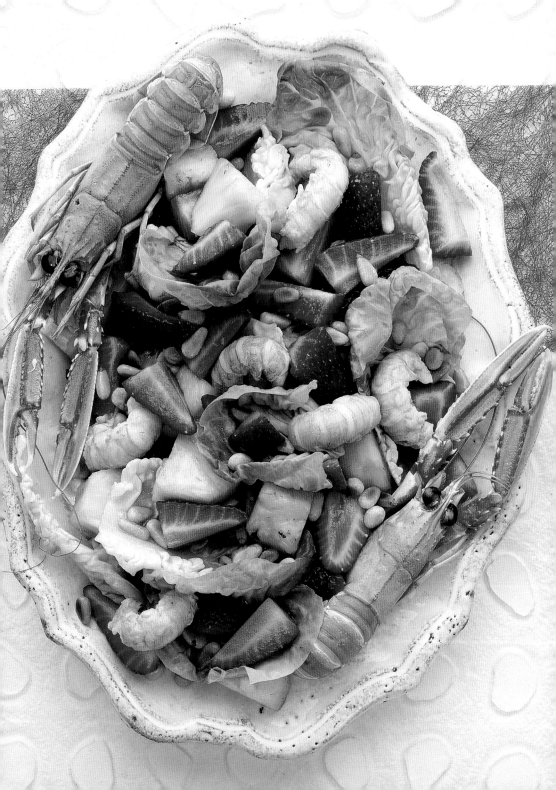

Sweet chilli prawn & egg noodle salad

Serves 4

2 blocks dried fine egg noodles
(about 130g)
4 celery sticks, finely sliced on the
diagonal
150g radishes, thinly sliced

300g beansprouts
400g cooked and peeled king prawns
4 tbsp sweet chilli sauce, plus more
to serve
salt and freshly ground black pepper

1. Put the egg noodles in a large bowl. Pour over a kettle of boiling water
and cover with clingfilm. Set aside for 5 minutes, stirring halfway, until just
softened. Drain, run under cold water to cool, then drain again and tip into
a large bowl.

2. Add the celery, radishes, beansprouts and king prawns to the noodles.

3. Drizzle with sweet chilli sauce, season and toss everything together until
combined. Divide between plates and serve with extra sweet chilli sauce to
drizzle over.

Razor clams & blood oranges

Serves 2

12 fresh razor clams
1 garlic clove, finely sliced
3 tbsp olive oil
2 tbsp red wine vinegar
1 red onion, very finely sliced
1 large fennel bulb, trimmed and
   very thinly sliced

1 tbsp small capers, rinsed and
   drained (optional)
2 blood oranges
100g purple or Kalamata olives
20g bunch of fresh flat-leaf parsley,
   leaves removed
salt and freshly ground black pepper

1. Heat the grill. Wash the clams under cold running water then lay them on a roasting tray and give them a quick turn under the hot grill for a minute or so. This should nudge open the shells. Remove them from the grill.

2. As soon as they are cool enough to handle, take out the long, white, meaty clam. Cut off the digger (the dark bit at the end) as it is invariably gritty. You might also snip the clam open lengthways to check for sand. Once they are clean, the clams can be returned to the grill, back in the shell. After another 2 minutes of cooking they should be ready. Reserve the juices, then slice the clams. Set aside.

3. In a large bowl, combine the clam juices with the garlic, olive oil, vinegar and ½ tsp salt. Fold in the clams, onion, fennel and capers, if using. Set aside for 30 minutes. You could chill it for a couple of days. On its own, it's a good tapa or antipasto dish.

4. Cut the top and bottom off the oranges and place flat-side down on a chopping board. Run a fruit or paring knife down the peel – working just beneath the pith – from top to bottom and all around each orange. Segment or slice into cross-sections. Add the pieces of orange, olives and parsley to the salad. Check the seasoning and serve.

If you can't get hold of any razor clams, use 300g squid instead.

Sweet potato, orange & mussel salad

Illustrated on the following pages

Serves 2

2 large sweet potatoes, cut lengthways into thick slices

4 tbsp olive oil

1kg live mussels, cleaned and debearded (discard open ones that do not close when tapped, and any with cracked shells)

1 small red onion or shallot, finely chopped

1–2 tbsp Seville orange juice

2 tbsp chopped fresh parsley

pinch of caster sugar (optional)

1 large or 2 small chicory, separated into leaves

1 small fennel bulb, trimmed and very finely sliced (feathery tops reserved)

2 sweet oranges, peel and pith removed, sliced or segmented

salt and freshly ground black pepper

1. Heat the grill to high, or use a ridged cast-iron grill pan. Brush the sweet potatoes with 1 tbsp of the oil, season, then grill until browned and tender. Cool a little then cut into strips and put in a large bowl.

2. Meanwhile, steam the mussels in a pan over boiling water until the shells open. (Discard any mussels that aren't open after 5–6 minutes' steaming.)

3. Add the shelled mussels (reserve a few shells) to the sweet potato with the onion, remaining oil, orange juice and parsley.

4. Toss to mix and season to taste with salt, pepper and maybe a pinch or two of sugar.

5. Just before serving, toss in the chicory, fennel and orange slices and any chopped feathery fennel tops. Serve immediately, garnished with a few of the reserved mussel shells.

The sharp Seville orange juice contrasts well with the sweet orange slices. If you are unable to find it, use sweet orange juice with a squeeze of lime or lemon to sharpen things up.

Crab, avocado & pink grapefruit salad

Serves 4
55ml olive oil
juice of 1 lemon
100g rocket leaves
2 medium avocados, sliced

1 pink grapefruit, peeled and
  segmented
3 whole crabs, white meat only
salt and freshly ground black pepper
10 chives, snipped, to serve

1. In a small bowl, mix together the oil, lemon juice and a little seasoning.
2. In another bowl combine the rocket, avocado, grapefruit and crabmeat.
To serve, divide between four plates, drizzle with the dressing and garnish
with the snipped chives.

Good quality pink grapefruit will have a
smooth, firm and shiny skin. Choose a fruit
that is medium to large and heavy for its size.

Seafood salad with lime & chilli salsa

Illustrated on the following pages

Serves 6
large handful of fresh parsley
1kg live mussels, cleaned and
 debearded (discard open ones that
 do not close when tapped, and any
 with cracked shells)
500g raw tiger prawns, peeled and
 deveined with tail-shells on
300g fresh prepared squid, cleaned
 and cut into rings or strips
2 tbsp avocado oil

juice of 1 lime
1 small shallot, finely chopped
100g rocket leaves

For the lime and chilli salsa
finely grated zest of 1 lime
1 garlic clove
1 small red chilli, halved and
 deseeded
large handful fresh mint

1. Put 100ml of water in a large pan. Tear the stalks from the parsley
(reserve the leaves for making the salsa) and add to the pan with a couple of
black peppercorns. Bring to the boil, then add the mussels, cover and cook
for 5 minutes, shaking the pan until all the shells have opened. Remove the
mussels with a slotted spoon, discarding any that haven't opened.
2. Add the prawns and squid to the pan, cook for 2 minutes or so until both
are cooked. Remove with a slotted spoon.
3. Boil the liquid in the pan until reduced by half, then spoon about 3 tbsps
of it (avoid the pepper and stalks) into a bowl and leave to cool. Discard the
remaining liquid.
4. Whisk the avocado oil and lime juice into the reserved cooking liquid.
Season and stir in the shallot.
5. Shell the mussels and toss with the prawns and squid. Cover and chill.
6. To make the salsa, put the lime zest, garlic and chilli in a blender and
whiz until chopped. Add the mint and reserved parsley leaves and whiz to
make a fine mixture.
7. Toss together the seafood with the shallot dressing, then gently fold in the
rocket. Divide between serving bowls. Spoon over some lime and chilli salsa.

Smoked fish salad

Serves 4

125g hot smoked trout, flaked
225g smoked mackerel, flaked
125g hot smoked salmon, flaked
½ red onion, peeled and sliced
8 trimmed radishes, sliced
1 ripe avocado, peeled and cut into
  chunks
20g fresh chives, snipped

6 tbsps mustard dressing or French
  dressing (see the recipes
  on pages 165 or 264)
salt and freshly ground black pepper

To serve
crusty bread and butter to serve
50g baby spinach leaves

1. In a large serving bowl combine all the ingredients together – be careful
not to break up the fish pieces too much, you want them to be fairly chunky.
2. Pour over the dressing, season and serve with some crusty bread and
butter and a little baby spinach leaves on the side.

Warm salad of smoked salmon & pancetta

Serves 4

250g crispy mixed salad leaves
1 ripe avocado, diced
150g smoked salmon
130g cubed pancetta
6 tbsp French dressing (see the
    recipe on page 264)

1. Divide the salad leaves between serving plates, add the avocado and mix together carefully.
2. Tear the smoked salmon into rough strips and scatter over the plates.
3. Dry-fry the pancetta in a frying pan for 3–4 minutes until crisp, then add the honey and mustard dressing and let it bubble briefly. Spoon over each plate and serve immediately.

The combination of the smoked salmon with warm pancetta make this a satisfying and substantial main meal.

Peppered mackerel with vegetable crisps

Serves 2

3 tbsp extra-virgin olive oil

1 tbsp lemon juice

150g green beans

130g mixed salad leaves

2–3 smoked peppered mackerel fillets

150g cherry tomatoes, halved

40g crushed vegetable crisps

salt and freshly ground black pepper

1. Make a simple dressing by whisking the extra-virgin olive oil with the lemon juice, season and set aside.

2. Cook the beans in boiling salted water for 2–3 minutes, until just tender, then refresh under cold water, drain and cut in half.

3. Tip the salad leaves into a large bowl and add the beans.

4. Peel off the skin from 2–3 smoked peppered mackerel fillets and tear the flesh into bite-sized pieces. Add to the salad with the cherry tomatoes.

5. Add the dressing and toss well. Divide between large plates and scatter with a handful of crushed vegetable crisps to serve.

Herring with potato, beetroot & dill salad

Serves 2

250g new potatoes
75ml crème fraîche
1 dsp wholegrain mustard
1¼ tbsp fresh dill, snipped into
small sprigs

150g marinated herring with fresh
lemon
200g cocktail beetroot
salt and freshly ground black pepper

1. Halve or quarter any larger potatoes and cook them all in a pan of boiling salted water until tender.

2. Meanwhile, mix together the crème fraîche, mustard and dill (reserve a few sprigs to serve), and season with salt and pepper. Arrange the herring on two plates.

3. Drain the potatoes and then tip them into a bowl and, while still hot, gently mix them with the beetroot and drizzle with the dressing. Serve with the herring and sprinkle over the reserved dill.

This will also work well using other oily fish, such as smoked trout or mackerel fillets.

Haddock, crispy bacon & spinach salad

Serves 4

3½ tbsp olive oil

8 slices smoked streaky bacon, cut into 1cm pieces

500g white haddock fillet, skin removed

4 eggs, at room temperature

1 tbsp white-wine vinegar

½ tsp wholegrain mustard

120g baby spinach leaves

salt and freshly ground black pepper

1. Heat a large non-stick frying pan and add 1½ tbsp of the oil. Put the bacon in the pan and cook over a high heat for 5–8 minutes, until crisp.

2. Remove with a slotted spoon onto kitchen paper and set aside.

3. Pour away a little of the oil, add the haddock to the pan and cook over a high heat for 4–5 minutes on each side, or until just cooked through.

4. Meanwhile, add the eggs to a pan of boiling water, return to the boil, then simmer for 4½ minutes. Drain the eggs, allow to cool slightly, then peel.

5. In a small bowl, mix the remaining oil, vinegar, mustard and seasoning and toss with the spinach leaves and crispy bacon. Divide between plates and put pieces of the haddock on the salad. Top with the soft-boiled egg, broken open with a knife, and serve.

salads
chicken, duck & game

Chicken, red onion & green beans

Serves 4

350g fine green beans, trimmed

5–6 tbsps olive oil

2 medium red onions, peeled and
    each cut into 8 wedges

4 chicken breasts, skins removed
    and sliced into strips

juice of 1 lemon

2 tbsp small capers, rinsed

50g wild rocket leaves

80g fresh shaved Parmigiano
    Reggiano

salt and freshly ground black pepper

1. Preheat a griddle and bring a pan of salted water to the boil for the beans.

2. Brush the griddle with oil and cook the onions for a few minutes on each side. Meanwhile, cook the beans for 3–4 minutes or until tender. Drain and put in a large bowl. Mix with the cooked onions.

3. Season and griddle the chicken strips in 2 batches for 3–4 minutes on each side or until cooked through, adding more oil if needed.

4. Meanwhile, in another bowl, whisk together the lemon juice and 4 tbsps of olive oil, then add this mixture to the beans and onions. Add the chicken to the bowl as it is cooked. Toss everything together with the capers and rocket and arrange on four plates, scattering with parmesan.

Warm chicken, tomato, Feta & lemon salad

Serves 3

2 tbsp olive oil, plus a good splash
400g chicken breasts, cut into strips
1 garlic clove, crushed
1 small onion, finely sliced

200g cherry tomatoes, halved
zest of 1 lemon
squeeze of lemon juice
125g mixed salad leaves
150g Feta cheese

1. Heat a little olive oil in a large pan and stir-fry the chicken strips until tender. Remove and set aside.

2. Add the garlic and the onion to the chicken and stir-fry for 2–3 minutes, until softened.

3. Add the cherry tomatoes to the pan and stir-fry until they begin to wilt. Add the lemon zest, a squeeze of lemon juice and a good splash of olive oil. Return the chicken to the pan and toss it all together.

4. Divide the mixed salad between three plates and spoon over the chicken mixture. Crumble the Feta between the plates.

Smoked chicken & papaya salad

Illustrated on the following pages

Serves 4

1 tbsp sesame seeds

½ cucumber

2 ripe papayas

400g cooked smoked chicken
   breasts, skins removed

1 romaine lettuce heart

For the dressing

5cm piece fresh ginger

2 tsp rice or white-wine vinegar

2 tbsp light olive oil

1 tsp toasted sesame oil

salt and freshly ground black pepper

1. Heat a dry frying pan over a medium-high heat. Add the sesame seeds and dry-fry for 1–2 minutes, until lightly toasted. Tip into a bowl and set aside to cool.

2. Peel the cucumber, then cut in half lengthways and scoop out and discard the seeds with a teaspoon. Cut the cucumber into thin slices and set aside.

3. Peel, halve and deseed the papayas, then cut the flesh lengthways into thin slices. Cut the smoked chicken breasts lengthways into long thin slices.

4. Make the dressing. Finely grate the ginger onto a plate, then scoop up the pulp and squeeze the juice out into a small bowl. Discard the pulp. Add the vinegar, then gradually whisk in the olive and sesame oils and some salt and freshly ground black pepper to taste. Stir in half the toasted sesame seeds.

5. Shred the lettuce hearts and mix with the cucumber. Pile into the centre of four plates. Alternate slices of the papaya and smoked chicken on top, and drizzle with the dressing. Sprinkle with the rest of the sesame seeds to serve.

Chicken & mango with a chilli lime dressing

Serves 4
8 tbsp olive oil
juice of 1 lime
1 Thai red chilli, deseeded and
  chopped
3 tbsp roughly chopped fresh
  coriander

2 small ripe mangoes
4 chicken breasts
150g mixed salad leaves
salt and freshly ground black pepper

1. Make the dressing by mixing together 6 tbsp olive oil, lime juice, chilli and coriander. Season and set aside.
2. Meanwhile, cook the chicken. Heat a griddle pan to a medium heat. Brush the chicken breasts with the remaining 2 tbsp olive oil and when the griddle is hot place the chicken in the pan and cook for 6–8 minutes each side until charred and golden and the chicken cooked through.
3. Peel the mangoes and cut into slices. Slice the chicken diagonally into thick strips.
4. Divide the salad between four plates and top with the mango and chicken slices. Drizzle over the dressing to serve.

The chilli in this dressing is a perfect match with the sweet mango. If you prefer a milder taste, use larger red chillies.

Chicken, asparagus & avocado salad

Serves 2

250g asparagus, trimmed
2 chicken breasts, skins removed
generous pinch dried chilli flakes
3 tbsp chopped fresh flat-leaf parsley
200g natural yogurt

1 tbsp vegetable oil
1 avocado, peeled and chopped
120g baby spinach leaves
50g rocket leaves
2 tbsp hemp seeds
salt and freshly ground black pepper

1. Simmer the asparagus for 2–3 minutes in salted water in a frying pan, then drain and cut the spears in half. Dry the pan.

2. Place the chicken between layers of clingfilm and flatten with a rolling pin. Season with salt and chilli. Mix the parsley into the yogurt and season.

3. Heat the oil in the pan and fry the chicken for 3–4 minutes on each side over a medium-high heat until cooked through.

4. Slice the chicken, toss with the asparagus, avocado, spinach, rocket and a drizzle of the pan juices. Scatter with hemp seeds and serve with the yogurt.

Crispy chilli chicken salad

Serves 2

¼ cucumber

2 spring onions, finely shredded

2 cooked, skinless chicken breasts

2 tbsp olive oil

2 tbsp hot chilli relish

juice of 1 lime

1 tbsp chopped fresh coriander

1 Little Gem lettuce, leaves separated

2 spring onions, finely shredded

1 lime, cut into wedges, to serve

salt and freshly ground black pepper

1. Scrape out and discard the seeds from the cucumber using a teaspoon. Chop and set aside.

2. Tear the chicken into bite-sized pieces. Heat a pan until hot, then add the olive oil. Fry the chicken for 5 minutes, stirring, until it is hot and crispy at the edges.

3. Take off the heat and stir through the chilli relish and lime juice. Put into a bowl, toss with the cucumber and coriander. Season to taste.

4. Serve on Little Gem lettuce leaves topped with the shredded spring onions and lime wedges.

Chicken noodle salad with ginger & peanuts

Serves 2

2 chicken breasts, preferably with skins on

3 tsp grated fresh ginger

grated zest of 1 lime

2 tbsp groundnut or sunflower oil

2 garlic cloves, finely chopped

1 green chilli, deseeded and finely chopped

3 tbsp crunchy peanut butter

2 tsp Thai fish sauce or light soy sauce

1 kaffir lime leaf, finely shredded

2 globes of preserved stem ginger in syrup, drained and chopped

lime juice, to taste

brown sugar, to taste

100–120g thin or thick rice noodles

small handful of fresh coriander

225g carrots, cut into long shreds

1 small green or red pepper, cut into long shreds

10 cm piece cucumber, seeded and cut into long, thin shreds

2–3 tbsp roasted peanuts, roughly chopped

1. Slash the skin of the chicken with a sharp knife. Mix together half the ginger, the lime zest and 1 tbsp oil. Rub into the chicken, cover and marinate in the fridge for at least an hour.

2. Meanwhile, roast or cook the chicken; 7–8 minutes on each side under the grill; 20–25 minutes at 180°C (fan 160°C), gas 4 to roast. Allow to cool a little then slice or shred into bite-sized pieces.

3. While the chicken is cooking, make the dressing. In a small pan, heat the remaining oil and gently cook the remaining ginger, with the garlic and chilli for a few minutes – don't let it brown. Remove from the heat and stir in the peanut butter; let it melt. Stir in 4–6 tbsp water to make a thick, creamy dressing and reheat a little. Add the Thai fish sauce or soy sauce, kaffir lime leaf, chopped stem ginger, lime juice and sugar to taste. Let it bubble gently for a few more minutes. Thin down with 2–3 tablespoons more water to make a spoonable dressing. Chop the coriander stalks and stir in.

4. Cook the noodles according to packet instructions. Drain, rinse and leave in a bowl of iced water until ready to serve.

5. Drain the noodles and divide between two shallow bowls. Place the shredded vegetables and most of the coriander leaves on top, followed by the still-warm chicken. Spoon the dressing over and scatter with more coriander and the chopped roasted peanuts.

Chicken with croûtons & Gorgonzola dressing

Serves 4-6

1 ready-to-eat chicken
150g baby spinach leaves
2 handfuls of croûtons (see page 59)
250g baby plum tomatoes, halved

100g Gorgonzola cheese, crumbled,
  plus more to garnish
125g plain yogurt
1–2 tbsp of lemon juice
salt and freshly ground black pepper

1. Tear the cooked chicken into bite-sized pieces. Put the spinach leaves into a large bowl and add the torn chicken meat. Add a couple of handfuls of croûtons and the halved plum tomatoes. Toss together lightly.

2. Beat together the Gorgonzola, yogurt, lemon juice and some seasoning.

3. Divide the salad between plates and spoon over the dressing. Scatter with a little more cheese to serve.

Creamy Gogonzola dressing with crunchy croûtons and juicy tomatoes make this a wonderfully varied combination of textures.

Moroccan chicken & potato salad

Serves 6

750g waxy new potatoes
1 tbsp fresh lemon juice
6 tbsp extra-virgin olive oil
2 tbsp chopped fresh mint
2 red chillies, deseeded and finely
    chopped

120g spring onions, chopped
1 tsp Spanish smoked paprika
4 large chicken breasts, skins
    removed and cut into wide strips
salt and freshly ground black pepper

1. Cook the potatoes in boiling salted water for 12–15 minutes, until just tender. Drain well and quarter each potato. Put into a large bowl.

2. Whisk together the lemon juice, 4 tbsp oil, the mint and chillies. Season with salt and pepper. Pour over the potatoes then leave to cool. Stir in the spring onions.

3. Mix the remaining oil with the paprika. Add the chicken and mix well.

4. Preheat the grill. Lay out the chicken on a foil-lined tray and cook under the grill for 8–10 minutes, turning once. Toss the chicken with the potato salad and serve.

This makes a wonderful al fresco lunch and is great for the barbecue. Cook the chicken for 8–10 minutes and mix with the potato salad.

Chicken & crunchy tortilla salad

Serves 2

130g mixed salad leaves
1 cooked chicken breast, shredded
1 crisp red onion, sliced
2 handfuls of spicy tortilla chips
125g baby plum tomatoes, quartered
3 tbsp roasted red pepper dressing
3 tbsp crème fraîche or soured cream

1. Divide the salad leaves between two bowls and add the shredded chicken.
2. Scatter a few slices of red onion over the top and add the tortilla chips and quartered tomatoes.
3. Make an instant salad dressing by mixing together equal quantities of roasted red pepper dressing and crème fraîche or soured cream. Drizzle over the salad and serve.

For an alternative dressing, whiz a few strips of roasted red peppers into some red-wine vinaigrette or use the Caesar salad dressing on page 274.

Warm chicken with tarragon mayonnaise

Serves 4

2 ripe avocados, halved, stoned,
   peeled and sliced
200g radishes, topped and tailed
   and sliced in half
200ml good quality mayonnaise
   (see the recipe on page 278)

4 tbsp chopped fresh tarragon,
   plus a few sprigs to serve
juice of 1 lime
1 ready-to-eat roasted chicken

1. Divide the avocado and radishes between four plates.

2. Mix the mayonnaise, chopped tarragon and enough lime juice to give a runny consistency.

3. Cut up the chicken into chunky pieces and divide between the plates.

4. Dollop a big spoonful of the tarragon mayonnaise onto each plate and garnish with a few tarragon sprigs.

Thai chicken salad

Serves 4

1 tbsp olive oil

450g chicken breasts, skins removed
and cut into bite-sized pieces

1 small onion, very finely chopped

2 garlic cloves, crushed

2 tbsp soy sauce, plus extra to serve

2 tsp caster sugar

1–2 Thai red chillies, deseeded and
very thinly sliced

1 cucumber

2 large carrots, cut into very thin
strips

150g beansprouts

3 tbsp coarsely chopped fresh mint

3 tbsp coarsely chopped fresh
coriander leaves

40g roasted salted peanuts, chopped
(optional)

grated zest and juice of 1 lime,
plus wedges to serve

1. Heat the olive oil in a wok or large frying pan and stir-fry the chicken
pieces over a high heat for 3-4 minutes. Add the chopped onion and garlic
and stir-fry for a further 2 minutes. Add the soy sauce, sugar and sliced
chillies and stir-fry for 3–4 minutes more, until the chicken is brown and
the sauce has reduced to a sticky glaze.

2. Meanwhile cut the cucumber in half lengthways, scoop out the seeds with
a teaspoon and discard, then slice on the diagonal. Toss with the chicken.
Add the remaining ingredients and stir to combine.

3. Serve with lime wedges to squeeze over, and extra soy sauce for drizzling.

Vietnamese minted chicken salad

Serves 4

2 carrots, grated

large handful fresh beansprouts

large handful fresh mint, plus extra
leaves to garnish

2 shallots, finely sliced

2 small red chillies, deseeded and
finely sliced, plus an extra sliced
chilli with seeds to garnish

3 cooked chicken breasts,
finely sliced

For the dressing

2 garlic cloves, crushed

2 tbsp brown sugar

1 tbsp rice vinegar

juice of 2 limes

1 tbsp fish sauce

4 tbsp vegetable oil

freshly ground black pepper

1. Put the carrot, beansprouts, mint leaves, shallots and chillies in a large
bowl and gently toss together. Set aside.

2. For the dressing, put the garlic, sugar, rice vinegar, lime juice, fish sauce,
vegetable oil and some freshly ground black pepper into a small bowl and
whisk together well.

3. Divide the salad between four bowls. Add the sliced chicken, toss well and
drizzle with the dressing. Garnish with the extra mint, chilli and seeds.

You can also use warm chicken in this dish.
Quickly stir-fry thin strips in a little olive oil
until lightly brown and crispy at the edges.

Five-spice duck salad with chicory & pears

Illustrated on the following pages

Serves 4

2 duck breasts

1 large ripe pear

2 small heads chicory, large
   leaves torn

120g herb salad

freshly ground black pepper

For the marinade

2 tbsps soy sauce

1 tbsp clear honey

½ tsp Chinese five-spice

freshly ground black pepper

For the dressing

3 tbsps extra-virgin olive oil

1 tbsp balsamic vinegar

1 tbsp soy sauce

1 clove garlic, peeled and finely
   chopped

2.5cm piece fresh ginger, peeled
   and finely chopped

½ tsp clear honey

juice of ½ lime

freshly ground black pepper

1. Using a sharp knife, score a diamond pattern into the duck breasts, then marinate them in the soy, honey, five-spice and some black pepper for at least 10 minutes but preferably a couple of hours, covered, in the fridge.

2. Preheat the oven to 200°C (fan 180°C), gas 6. Heat a non-stick frying pan until very hot. Wipe off as much of the marinade as you can from the chicken and place the breasts, skin-side down, in the pan. Sear them until they are brown. Turn the heat down to low and let the fat render out slowly (about 10 minutes). The skin on the duck breasts will end up crispy.

3. Place the duck on a baking tray and roast for 10 minutes, skin-side up, then let the breasts rest out of the oven for 10 minutes. Slice them thinly.

4. Place the dressing ingredients, together with a generous grinding of black pepper, in a lidded jar. Shake well to combine and set aside.

5. Peel, quarter and core the pear, then cut into thin slices. Season with freshly ground pepper.

6. Arrange the chicory and herb salad on four serving plates and divide the sliced duck and pears between them. Just before serving, shake the dressing again and drizzle over the salad.

Chinese duck, orange & noodle salad

Serves 4

125g dried medium egg noodles
2 tbsp toasted sesame oil
2 oranges
300g Chinese stir-fry vegetables
½ head shredded Chinese leaf
2 large duck breasts
1 tsp Chinese five-spice
salt and freshly ground black pepper

1. Cook the noodles in boiling water for 3–4 minutes. Drain well and tip into a large bowl. Toss with the sesame oil.

2. Cut off and discard skin and pith from the oranges. Segment the oranges into the bowl of noodles. Squeeze any excess juice from the membranes into the bowl. Add the stir-fry vegetables and the shredded Chinese leaf to the bowl. Toss everything together. Season to taste and set aside.

3. Heat a frying pan over a medium heat. Rub the duck breasts with the Chinese five-spice, then season. Cook for 5 minutes, then turn and cook for a further 5 minutes for pink meat, or longer if you like your meat well done. Lift onto a plate and leave to rest for 10 minutes.

4. Slice the duck on the diagonal. Divide the noodle salad between four plates and top with slices of duck breast.

Spiced pigeon with roast butternut squash

Serves 4

8 pigeon breasts
3 tbsp thick Greek yogurt
3 tbsp olive oil
½ tsp ground ginger
½ tsp ground cumin seeds
½ tsp salt
½ tsp hot paprika, preferably smoked

1 medium butternut squash (600g)
2 red onions, sliced
juice of 1 lemon
2 tbsp pumpkin seed oil or extra-
   virgin olive oil, plus extra to serve
handful of wild rocket leaves
2 tbsp butter
salt and freshly ground black pepper

1. Put the pigeon breasts, Greek yogurt, 1 tbsp olive oil, ginger, cumin, salt and paprika in a shallow ceramic dish and marinate for at least 2 hours, preferably overnight.

2. Preheat the oven to 200°C (fan 180°C), gas 6. Leaving the skin on, cut the squash into rings or half-moon slices, whichever is easiest. Toss the pieces in the remaining olive oil and add a little salt. Lay the slices, spaced well apart, on a baking sheet and cook in the oven for 25 minutes, or until slightly browned and crispy at the edges. (If you bake them this way the skin is very edible, like a jacket potato.)

3. Meanwhile, toss the sliced red onions in a bowl with the lemon juice and the pumpkin seed oil or extra-virgin olive oil. Season lightly. Gently mix the onion with the squash and rocket leaves to make a warm salad.

4. Heat the butter in a wide-based frying pan and sear the pigeon breasts for about 3 minutes on each side. Remove from the pan and set aside to rest for a good 5 minutes.

5. Cut each pigeon breast into three and serve with the butternut squash salad and extra pumpkin seed oil, if you like.

You could use duck breasts instead of pigeon. If you do, increase the total cooking time to about 10 minutes.

Pheasant, apple, fennel & orange salad

Serves 2–3

2 cold roasted pheasant breasts
1 small flavourful apple (Braeburn
  or Cox's)
½ bulb fennel, finely sliced
1 small orange
1 head chicory
85g watercress
50g walnut pieces

For the dressing

1 tsp grainy mustard
1 tsp runny honey
3 tbsps live natural yogurt
1½ tbsp cider vinegar
½ tsp ground coriander
55ml light olive oil
salt and freshly ground black pepper

1. To make the dressing, put the mustard, honey, vinegar and ground coriander in a bowl and whisk together. Gradually add the oil until you have a thick dressing. Now add the yogurt, whisk thoroughly and season with salt and black pepper.

2. Separate the leaves from the chicory and place them in a bowl of iced water. Score the orange skin into quarters with a sharp knife, place in a bowl and cover with boiling water. Leave for 2–3 minutes, then rinse with cold water. Remove skin and pith, and cut the orange into small segments.

3. Cut the pheasant breasts into strips. Drain the chicory and pat dry with kitchen paper. Quarter, core and slice the apple.

4. Arrange the watercress in a shallow serving bowl, scatter over half the chicory and fennel. Arrange pieces of pheasant, apple, orange, fennel and chicory alternately round the bowl. Finally, drizzle over half the dressing and scatter with walnut pieces. Serve the remainder of the dressing in a small jug for those who would like extra.

This recipe uses only the pheasant breasts. Save the legs and carcass to make a dark, rich stock that would be a great base for an onion or chestnut soup.

salads
veggie

Warm spinach, shallot & baby beetroot salad

Serves 4
250g shallots
2 tbsp extra-virgin olive oil
300g small raw beetroots, leaves
reserved to serve
4 large garlic cloves, thinly sliced
75g walnut pieces
350g baby spinach leaves, washed
and dried
2 medium fennel bulbs, trimmed and
thinly sliced
sea salt

For the pink peppercorn dressing
1 tsp dried pink peppercorns
1 tbsp cider vinegar
5 tbsp medium olive oil

1. Preheat the oven to 190°C (fan 170°C), gas 5. Toss the shallots with half the oil and a sprinkling of sea salt in a roasting tin. Roast for 30 minutes.
2. Meanwhile, put the beetroots into a saucepan of cold salted water and bring to the boil. Simmer for 15 minutes, or until just cooked, then drain and pop out of their skins.
3. After 30 minutes, add the garlic to the roasting shallots, drizzle with the remaining tbsp of oil and roast for a further 10 minutes.
4. Add the beetroots and walnuts to the tin, toss to coat in the oil and roast until the garlic is golden – a further 5–10 minutes.
5. Put the spinach in a large salad bowl and scatter with the fennel.
6. To make the dressing, crush the peppercorns and ¼ tsp of salt, and mix in the vinegar. Whisk in the olive oil a little at a time.
7. Spoon the shallots, garlic, walnuts and beetroots onto the spinach and fennel, and pour over the dressing. Add the beetroot leaves, toss everything well and serve while still warm.

If you can't find raw beetroot, use cooked baby beetroots (not in vinegar) and add to the roasting tin with the walnuts.

Little Gem, mushroom, apple & celery salad

Serves 4

3 celery sticks, thickly sliced diagonally, leaves reserved to serve

6 spring onions, finely shredded

4 Little Gem lettuces, cut in half lengthways

125g closed cup chestnut mushrooms, wiped clean and cut into 3 slices

2 tbsp extra-virgin olive oil

1 Cox's apple

salt and freshly ground black pepper

For the mustard dressing

1 tsp Dijon mustard

pinch of sugar

1 tbsp cider vinegar

4 tbsp extra-virgin olive oil

1. Put the celery leaves and shredded spring onions into a bowl of cold water. Put the Little Gem lettuce in another large bowl of cold water. This will help keep everything crisp.

2. To make the dressing, mix the mustard, sugar and vinegar in a small bowl, then season and whisk in the oil, a little at a time, until thick.

3. Sprinkle the sliced mushrooms with a little salt and black pepper. Heat the oil in a frying pan and, when hot, seal the mushrooms on both sides for about 1 minute. Tip into a large salad bowl and mix in 1 tbsp of the dressing. Leave to marinate for 15 minutes.

4. Cut the apple into quarters and core, then cut each quarter into 8 slices. Add the apple slices and celery to the mushrooms. Dry the Little Gem lettuce and mix into the salad.

5. Drain the celery leaves and spring onions, pat dry and fold half into the salad with the remaining dressing. Scatter the other half over the salad and serve immediately.

Couscous, broad beans, peas, mint & Feta

Serves 4–6
225g couscous
4–5 tbsp extra-virgin olive oil
225g fresh or frozen broad beans
225g fresh or frozen peas

4 plum tomatoes, deseeded and
  finely chopped
4 tbsp chopped fresh mint
150g Feta, crumbled
salt and freshly ground black pepper

1. Put the couscous into a large bowl and gradually stir in 300ml warm water until it is all absorbed. Leave to stand for 10–15 minutes until the grains are tender and plump.

2. Stir in 1 tbsp olive oil and rub the grains between your fingers to break up any lumps.

3. Cook the broad beans and peas in boiling salted water for 5–6 minutes, until just tender. Refresh under cold running water. Drain well and remove the tough outer skin from the broad beans. Add the beans and peas to the couscous and stir together.

4. Stir in the tomatoes and chopped mint. Season the remaining olive oil well and pour over the couscous, using a fork to distribute it. Stir in the Feta. Spoon into separate bowls or on to a platter and serve.

Mediterranean vegetable salad

Serves 6

4 medium courgettes, thickly sliced

3 red peppers, halved, deseeded and
cut into wide strips

1 tbsp vegetable oil, for tossing

500g baby plum tomatoes, halved

125g rocket leaves

150g baby spinach leaves

salt and freshly ground black pepper

For the dressing

6 tbsp extra-virgin olive oil

2 tbsp white wine vinegar

½ tsp Dijon mustard

pinch of sugar

salt and freshly ground black pepper

1. Put the courgettes and peppers into a large bowl and drizzle with a little vegetable oil. Season well and toss to coat thoroughly. Heat a griddle pan and cook the vegetables for 8–10 minutes, turning once. Transfer to a large bowl and set aside to cool.

2. Meanwhile, make the dressing by whisking all the ingredients together with plenty of seasoning.

3. Add the tomatoes, rocket and spinach to the bowl with the vegetables and toss well. Drizzle with the dressing and toss well again.

This makes a great summer salad. Instead of using a griddle you could barbecue the vegetables over a direct heat for 8-10 minutes, turning halfway through cooking.

New potato, sun-dried tomato & olive salad

Serves 8

750g waxy new potatoes
juice of 1 small lemon
6 tbsp extra-virgin olive oil
2 handfuls fresh chives, snipped
6 sun-dried tomatoes, thinly sliced
15 pitted whole black olives
salt and freshly ground black pepper

1. Cook the potatoes in boiling salted water for 12–15 minutes, until just tender. Drain well, and leave until cool enough to handle. Halve lengthways.
2. Put the lemon juice, olive oil, chives and plenty of seasoning into a large serving bowl and whisk.
3. Add the potatoes, toss and set aside to cool. Stir the tomatoes and olives through to serve.

This is the kind of salad that can be eaten all year round. The potatoes make it into a substantial dish while the sun-dried tomatoes add a touch of luxury.

Potato, watercress & apple salad

Serves 6

1kg new potatoes
5 tbsp pine nuts
3 tbsp pumpkin seeds
325g low-fat natural yogurt
zest of 1 lemon
2½ tbsp lemon juice

2 tbsp manuka or other clear honey
2 cored and diced eating apples
2 handfuls watercress leaves
  (stalks discarded)
1 stick celery, sliced
salt and freshly ground black pepper

1. Halve the new potatoes (or cut into three if large) and simmer in salted water for 10–15 minutes until tender. Drain and cool.

2. Heat a frying pan and when it is hot toast the pine nuts with the pumpkin seeds, until golden.

3. In a large bowl, mix together the yogurt, lemon zest, 1½ tbsp lemon juice and the honey. Stir in the potatoes, pine nuts and pumpkin seeds. Toss the apple in the remaining 1 tbsp lemon juice, add to the potato and mix well.

4. Add the watercress leaves and celery. Season well and serve.

Roast pepper & garlic salad with hazelnuts

Serves 4

2 large red peppers
2 large yellow peppers
1 large garlic bulb, cloves whole
　and unpeeled
3 tbsp olive oil

1 tsp salt
2 handfuls oregano or marjoram,
　leaves picked
1 tbsp sherry or balsamic vinegar
100g whole hazelnuts

1. Preheat the oven to 200°C (fan 180°C), gas 6. Cut the peppers lengthways into rough quarters, discarding any seeds and pith, but leaving the stalks on. Lay them on baking trays skin-side up.

2. Scatter the peppers with garlic, olive oil, salt, oregano and sherry or balsamic vinegar, and cover with foil. Roast for 20 minutes.

3. Remove the foil and return to the oven for another 15 minutes, or until wilted – their skins should be brown and wrinkly. (Leave the oven on to roast the nuts.) Set aside for at least 15 minutes.

4. Meanwhile, spread the hazelnuts in a single layer on a baking sheet and cook in the oven for 5 minutes until golden. Remove and cool slightly, then roughly crush in a pestle and mortar.

5. Transfer the peppers, garlic and the juices to a serving bowl, then scatter the lightly crushed nuts over the top. Squeeze the garlic out of its skin with your fingers as you eat the salad.

This dish is great on its own or served with a softish, mildish cheese or some oily fish such as mackerel.

Mangetout & avocado salad

Serves 4, generously
300g mangetout, trimmed
2 avocados
juice of 1 lemon
4 tbsp extra-virgin olive oil
1 tbsp Dijon mustard
1 red onion, thinly sliced

100g sun-blushed tomatoes
1 tbsp chopped fresh mint or
   tarragon
2 handfuls of pea shoots
3 tbsp pumpkin or sunflower seeds
salt and freshly ground black pepper

1. Blanch the mangetout in water that is at a rolling boil for no longer than 30 seconds. Set aside on kitchen paper to soak up the excess moisture.
2. While they rest, prepare the avocados. Halve lengthways and remove the stones. Using a small knife – a paring or fruit knife is ideal – cut criss-cross shapes through the flesh, stopping just short of the skin. Now you can simply peel the avocado over the salad bowl and let the pieces fall in.
3. Mix the lemon juice with the oil and mustard and dress the avocado pieces immediately. When ready to eat, add the other ingredients and toss lightly. Season to taste and serve.

This recipe has used mangetout (snow peas) but could be made just as easily with sugar snaps or raw, fresh broad beans.

Greek salad

Serves 6

1 cucumber, halved lengthways,
  deseeded and diced
1 large onion, thinly sliced
6 plum tomatoes, cut into chunks
24 pitted Greek black olives, halved
225g Feta, diced
1 head cos lettuce, roughly torn

For the dressing

2 tbsp fresh lemon juice
6 tbsp extra-virgin olive oil
1 garlic clove
2 tbsp fresh oregano or thyme
salt and freshly ground black pepper

1. Put the diced cucumber, onion, tomatoes, olives and Feta into a large serving bowl. Toss in the torn lettuce leaves.

2. Whisk the dressing ingredients together with plenty of seasoning and pour over the Greek salad to serve.

This is such a simple, fresh salad that can be made in next to no time. Source some really good quality ripe tomatoes as they will have a sweet, rich flavour.

Roasted baby vegetable salad with croûtons

Serves 2–3

1 red onion, cut into wedges
75g baby carrots
75g baby sweetcorn
6 tbsp olive oil
½ garlic and rosemary flatbread
1 tbsp red-wine vinegar
120g herb leaf salad
75g mangetout
salt and freshly ground black pepper

1. Preheat the oven to 220°C (fan 200°C), gas 7. Put the red onion wedges into a roasting tin. Add the carrots and sweetcorn (halve them if they are quite large). Drizzle with 2 tbsp olive oil, season and toss together. Roast for 20 minutes, turning halfway, until just tender.

2. Tear the garlic and rosemary flatbread into chunky croûtons, add these to the vegetables then toss together. Roast for a further 8–10 minutes, until the vegetables are lightly charred and the croûtons crisp.

3. Meanwhile, whisk together the remaining 4 tbsp olive oil, the red-wine vinegar and some seasoning.

4. Put the herb leaf salad into a large serving bowl, along with the reserved mangetout. Add the roasted vegetables and croûtons, drizzle with the dressing and gently toss together. Divide between bowls to serve.

Grilled spring onions, radish & cottage cheese

Serves 4
250g cottage cheese
120g spring onions
extra-virgin olive oil, for drizzling
1 small cucumber
1 small cos lettuce or 2 Little Gem,
  washed and roughly shredded
200g small radishes
12 whole mint leaves
salt

For the dressing
juice of 1 lemon, plus a little zest
3 tbsp extra-virgin olive oil
1 tsp Dijon mustard
salt and freshly ground black pepper

1. Drain the cottage cheese in a sieve to get rid of any excess whey.
2. Meanwhile, trim the spring onions of any wilted greens. Heat a frying
pan or griddle and dry-fry them for about 30 seconds to 1 minute each side.
Drizzle with olive oil and season with salt. Set aside on a plate.
3. Make the dressing by whisking all the ingredients together in a small
bowl. Season well and set aside.
4. Peel and halve the cucumber lengthways. Run a teaspoon along the seed
cavity to remove the seeds and discard. Finely slice the cucumber, then toss
together with the lettuce, radishes, spring onions, mint and dressing.
Scatter the cottage cheese curds over the salad to serve.

Look out for the flamboyant French breakfast
radish: bright pink with a white strip at the
base. If the leaves look fresh, toss them into
the salad as well – they taste like rocket.
This is great stuffed into pitta.

Griddled vegetables with mozzarella

Serves 4

1 courgette, cut into 1cm slices on the diagonal

1 small aubergine, cut into 1cm slices on the diagonal

2 peppers, deseeded and cut into wedges

4 artichoke hearts, drained and halved

1 tbsp olive oil

300g buffalo mozzarella, drained and sliced

salt and freshly ground black pepper

For the dressing

6 tbsp roughly chopped fresh basil, with 8 leaves reserved to garnish

3 tbsp olive oil

½ tbsp red-wine vinegar

½ tsp Dijon mustard

sea salt and freshly ground black pepper

1. Put the courgettes, aubergines, peppers and artichokes into a bowl, season and toss with the olive oil.

2. Heat a griddle pan until very hot, then cook the vegetables in batches, turning once griddle marks show on each side.

3. In a blender or using a pestle and mortar, whiz or pound the chopped basil with the oil, vinegar, mustard and some sea salt and some freshly ground black pepper.

4. Arrange the mozzarella and griddled vegetables on plates and drizzle the basil dressing over. Sprinkle with the remaining basil leaves.

Warm veg salad

Serves 4

1kg butternut squash

1 red onion, cut into 8 wedges

2 peppers, deseeded and cut into
large pieces

1 tbsp fresh thyme leaves, plus extra
sprigs to garnish

1 large garlic clove, crushed

2 tbsp olive oil

50g wild rocket leaves

1 tbsp balsamic glaze

100g Feta, crumbled

1. Preheat the oven to 200°C (fan 180°C), gas 6. Peel and deseed the squash and cut into eight thick wedges or large chunks. Put into a roasting tin with the onion and peppers. Add the thyme leaves, garlic and olive oil and toss well to coat. Pop the roasting tin in the oven for 45 minutes, or until the vegetables are tender and lightly charred.

2. Transfer the vegetables (including any juices) to a large serving bowl. Toss through the wild rocket and balsamic glaze.

3. To serve, divide the warm salad between four plates and scatter the crumbled Feta over the top. Garnish with the extra thyme.

Any leftover squash makes a great addition to mashed potatoes. Boil it with the potatoes, drain, and mash with some seasoning and grated Parmesan.

Five bean salad with shallot & quails' eggs

Illustrated on the following pages

Serves 4

125g mung beans, soaked overnight

200g frozen broad beans

2 shallots, sliced

juice of ½ lemon

150g fine green beans

150g Romano beans or stringless
    green beans, sliced diagonally

410g can red kidney beans, rinsed

12 quails' eggs, hard-boiled and
    halved (optional)

4 wheat tortillas, cut into wedges,
    to serve

a little sea salt

For the dressing

1 banana shallot or 2 round shallots,
    finely chopped

juice of ½ lemon

3 tbsp extra-virgin olive oil

1 large mild green chill, deseeded
    and finely chopped

1. Drain the mung beans and place in a large pan of fresh cold water.
Bring to the boil and simmer for 10 minutes, then add a little salt and cook
for a further 5 minutes, or until tender. Drain and set aside until needed.

2. Boil the broad beans in salted water for 4–5 minutes, until tender, then
drain and plunge into cold water. Drain again, then remove and discard the
tough white skins to reveal the bright green beans. Set aside.

3. Put the sliced shallots into a bowl with the lemon juice and set aside.

4. Meanwhile, make the dressing. Put the chopped shallot and lemon juice
into a large salad bowl and leave for 10 minutes. Whisk the oil into the
shallots, a little at a time, then stir in the chilli and a little sea salt to taste.

5. Add the mung and broad beans to the dressing and mix together.

6. Put the green and Romano beans into a pan of boiling salted water and
simmer for 4 minutes. Drain and refresh under cold water. Add to the salad
with the kidney beans and mix together.

7. Drain, rinse and dry the sliced shallots, then top the salad with the
shallots and quails' eggs, if using. Brown the tortilla wedges on a griddle
pan and serve with the salad.

Runner bean, tomato & pesto salad

Serves 6

600g runner beans
50g pine nuts
180g cherry tomatoes, quartered
75g sun-blush tomatoes in oil,
   drained, cut into strips
25g rocket leaves
3 x 100g small goats' cheese rounds
12 thin slices French bread, cut on
   the diagonal from a baguette
olive oil, for drizzling

For the pesto dressing

½ tsp Dijon mustard
1 tsp white-wine vinegar
2 tbsp extra-virgin olive oil
2 tbsp fresh pesto
salt and freshly ground black pepper

1. Bring a pan of lightly salted water to the boil. Top and tail the runner beans, then remove the strings from each side. Cut on the diagonal into 1cm slices. Drop into the boiling water and cook for about 5 minutes or until just tender. Drain, refresh in cold water, and drain well again.

2. Preheat the grill to high. Pop the pine nuts onto a baking tray and toast under the grill for 2 minutes, until golden. Set aside to cool.

3. Mix the runner beans, cherry and sun-blush tomatoes, pine nuts and rocket together in a bowl.

4. Make the dressing. Whisk the mustard and vinegar together, then slowly whisk in the oil. Stir in the pesto and season.

5. Discard the top and bottom of each cheese round and cut each into four slices. Grill the bread slices for 2 minutes. Turn over and grill for 1 minute, then drizzle with a little oil. Top each with a cheese slice, and grill until just beginning to melt.

6. Toss the dressing into the salad and spoon onto plates. Lay two warm cheese croûtes alongside each salad to serve.

This has a lovely combination of textures with crisp, fresh salad and the warm creamy goats' cheese croûtes.

salads
sides

Herb leaf salad

Serves 4–6

50g fresh flat-leaf parsley, all stems
removed

50g fresh chives, chopped into
lengths

50g fresh tarragon leaves, all stems
removed

50g fresh basil, all stems removed

2 tsp red-wine vinegar

1–2 tbsp extra-virgin olive oil

sea salt

1. Wash all the herbs and carefully dry them. Put them into a large serving bowl and mix together.

2. Whisk the red-wine vinegar into the olive oil and season with sea salt. Just before serving, drizzle over the leaves and toss.

This extremely simple but flavourful salad will complement almost any dish. Try it with lamb or grilled fish.

Red cabbage & beetroot salad

Illustrated on the following pages

Serves 4

3 plump garlic cloves, crushed

1 tbsp Dijon mustard

1 tbsp red-wine vinegar

3 tbsp extra-virgin olive oil

450g raw baby beetroot

100g shredded red cabbage

1 small bunch spring onions, shredded

2 tbsp chopped fresh parsley

1 tbsp poppy seeds

salt and freshly ground black pepper

1. Make the dressing. Put the garlic, mustard and red-wine vinegar into a bowl and whisk well. Gradually whisk in the olive oil and season generously. Set aside.

2. Peel the beetroot and grate using a grater or food processor. Put into a bowl with the shredded cabbage and spring onions, parsley and poppy seeds. Drizzle over the dressing and toss together using two forks.

Red cabbage and beetroot make a striking, colourful salad with strong flavours.

Salad with toasted mixed seeds

Serves 6

1 head radicchio
2 Little Gem lettuces or 1 cos lettuce
2 heads red or white chicory
150g radishes, trimmed and finely
    sliced
3 tbsp ready-toasted mixed seeds,
    such as sunflower, pumpkin and
    sesame
salt and freshly ground black pepper

For the dressing

4 tbsp olive oil
juice of 1 lime
1 tsp light muscovado sugar

1. Carefully break up all the salad leaves and the chicory. Wash well and dry.
Place in a large serving bowl and add the sliced radishes.

2. Mix all the ingredients for the dressing together and pour over the leaves.
Sprinkle with the toasted seeds and add a pinch of salt and plenty of freshly
ground black pepper. Toss well and serve.

This is a crunchy salad that will add interest
to simple chicken and fish dishes, and the
lime dressing is wonderfully refreshing.

Warm barley salad with butternut squash

Illustrated on the following pages

Serves 4

1 large butternut squash, peeled, deseeded and cut into 3cm-cubes

2 tbsp olive oil

250g pearl barley

200g fine green beans, trimmed and halved

1 medium red onion, peeled and finely diced

3 stalks celery heart, finely sliced

3 tbsp roughly chopped fresh mint leaves

4 tbsp roughly chopped fresh parsley

100g goats' cheese

salt and freshly ground black pepper

For the dressing

8 tbsp extra-virgin olive oil

1 clove garlic, peeled and finely chopped

½ tbsp dried crushed chillies

6 tbsp red-wine vinegar

1 tbsp runny honey

salt and freshly ground black pepper

1. Preheat the oven to 180°C (fan 160°C), gas 4. Spread the pieces of squash over a baking tray, drizzle with the olive oil and season. Bake in the oven for 20 minutes, remove and set aside.

2. Meanwhile, rinse the barley, then cook in plenty of boiling, salted water for about 20–25 minutes, or until just tender. In a separate pan, cook the beans in boiling water for 3–4 minutes.

3. To make the dressing, warm the oil in a pan, add the garlic and chilli and lightly brown over a low heat. Allow to cool slightly, then add the red-wine vinegar, honey and some seasoning. Whisk until combined.

4. Drain the barley and beans and place in a large bowl. Add the onion, celery and cooled squash. Pour the dressing over the salad and gently mix together. Add the herbs, mix again, then crumble the goats' cheese on top.

Courgette som tam

Serves 4

2 medium courgettes, trimmed

1 medium carrot, trimmed

100g French green beans, topped
  and tailed

2 garlic cloves, chopped

1–2 small red chillies, deseeded
  and sliced lengthways

salt and freshly ground black pepper

For the dressing

2 tbsp Thai fish sauce

juice of 2 limes

1 tsp sugar or honey

salt and freshly ground black pepper

To serve

1 large handful fresh coriander
  leaves, as a garnish

100g roasted peanuts, roughly
  crushed

1. Using a potato peeler, peel the courgettes along their length, then keep going, making strips of the flesh until you reach the seed pod in the centre. Discard the seed pod. Peel the carrot in the same way. Put the vegetables in a large bowl.

2. Blanch the green beans in plenty of boiling salted water for no longer than a couple of minutes, until they are just tender. Drain and rinse in cold water. Add to the bowl of vegetables, along with the chopped garlic and sliced chilli.

3. Make the dressing. Mix the fish sauce, lime juice and sugar, then season to taste. Pour the dressing over the vegetables, toss together and allow the salad to sit for a good 30 minutes before serving – this will deepen the flavour and have the effect of slightly 'cooking' the carrot and courgette.

4. Divide the salad between plates. Garnish with coriander leaves and serve with the crushed peanuts separately to sprinkle over.

This would be lovely as part of a Thai-style spread, but it also goes very well with simple grilled fish or chicken dishes.

Hot potato, orange & red cabbage salad

Serves 6

400g new potatoes, scrubbed

3 blood oranges or 2 medium oranges

¼ tsp of salt

½ tsp white-wine vinegar

4 tbsp mild olive oil

1 small or ½ medium red cabbage

1 medium red onion or 1 large pink shallot, sliced into thin wedges

2 white or pink chicory

1 tbsp flat-leaf parsley, leaves removed

1. Put the potatoes into a large saucepan of cold salted water and bring to the boil. Simmer for about 12–15 minutes, or until tender.

2. Meanwhile, finely grate ¼ tsp of zest from 1 orange and set aside. Cut the peel and pith from all the oranges and segment them over a bowl to catch all the juice. Squeeze in the juice from the remaining orange membranes and set aside.

3. Put the grated orange zest, white-wine vinegar and 2 tbsp of the reserved orange juice into a large salad bowl. Whisk in the oil a little at a time, then add the orange segments.

4. Shred the cabbage into another bowl, add the red onion or shallot wedges and toss well with the remaining orange juice.

5. Drain the cooked potatoes and cut into bite-sized pieces. Toss with the dressing and oranges in the salad bowl. Drain the cabbage and shallot wedges and add to the salad bowl.

6. Cut the chicory into bite-sized pieces and add to the salad bowl. Drain and dry the parsley leaves and add to the salad. Toss well and serve while the potatoes are still hot.

New potatoes with chorizo & broad beans

Illustrated on the previous pages

Serves 4

500g Jersey Royal new potatoes

1kg broad beans to yield about
200g podded beans

2 tbsp olive oil

1 medium onion, peeled and sliced

225g chorizo de pueblo, rind
removed and sliced into 1cm pieces

2 plum tomatoes, deseeded and
chopped

4 tbsp chopped flat-leaf parsley
leaves

2 tbsp sherry vinegar

2 handfuls rocket leaves

salt and freshly ground black pepper

1. Bring a large pan of salted water to the boil and cook the new potatoes for 10 minutes. Add the broad beans and cook for a further 3–5 minutes.

2. Meanwhile, heat the olive oil in a frying pan and soften the sliced onion for 3–4 minutes before adding the chorizo. Cook for a further 3 minutes, tossing to cook on both sides.

3. Drain the potatoes and beans, cool slightly, then thickly slice the potatoes lengthways and add to the onion mixture along with the beans, tomatoes, parsley and vinegar. Season and toss together. Add the rocket and toss once more before serving.

Serve this with some grilled or barbecued chicken or fish to make a hearty meal.

Braised peas with leeks, lettuce & mint

Serves 6

3 Little Gem lettuces or 5 Little Gem
   lettuce hearts
75g butter
2 small (about 150g) leeks, trimmed,
   washed and thinly sliced

750g frozen or freshly shelled peas
1 tbsp chopped fresh mint leaves
salt and freshly ground black pepper

1. Trim the lettuces and cut each lettuce lengthways into six wedges.

2. Melt half the butter in a deep sauté pan over a medium-low heat. Add the leeks and sauté gently for two minutes or until softened. Add the lettuces and cook for 1–2 minutes or until they begin to wilt. Add the peas and 100ml water. Season. Simmer for 3–4 minutes, stirring, until the peas are softened and about half the liquid has evaporated.

3. Dot over the remaining butter, sprinkle with the chopped mint and shake the pan briefly.

Warm pea & lentil salad

Serves 4
200g Puy lentils
2 garlic cloves
1 shallot or small onion, finely sliced
juice of 1 lemon or 2 limes
4 tbsp extra-virgin olive oil
200g peas

1. There is no need to soak Puy lentils. Just wash them and cook in plenty of unsalted water with the garlic for about 20 minutes, until they are tender but retaining some bite. You can discard the garlic at this point if you wish. Drain the lentils and place in a large serving bowl.
2. Add the shallot, lemon or lime juice and oil to the lentils and toss together. Season to taste and set aside.
3. Blanch the peas for no more than a minute or so in plenty of boiling water. Drain, add to the lentils and serve.

Try wilting some fresh herbs, such as basil, parsley, chives or mint into the salad. Toss them through the lentils before serving. You can use mangetout (snow peas), broad beans or sugar snaps instead of the peas.

Puttanesca tomatoes

Serves 2–3

500g ripe plum tomatoes
2 large cloves garlic, peeled
3 anchovy fillets, drained
8 pitted black olives

1 medium-sized red chilli
2 tsp small capers, drained
olive oil, for drizzling
2 tbsps freshly grated Parmesan
freshly ground black pepper

1. Preheat the oven to 190°C (fan 175°C), gas 5. Halve the tomatoes lengthways and place cut-side up on a baking tray in a single layer.
2. Finely chop the garlic, anchovy fillets, olives and chilli (there is no need to remove the seeds) and mix together in a bowl. Divide the mixture between the tops of the tomato halves, then scatter a few capers on to each one and season with pepper.
3. Drizzle with oil and roast on the centre shelf for 40 minutes, then scatter the Parmesan over the tomato halves and return to the oven for 5 minutes.

Eat this as is with some fresh crusty bread, or serve it alongside lamb, steak or chicken.

Tomato & sweet pickled pepper salad

Illustrated on the following pages

Serves 6
1 red onion, thinly sliced
1 tsp light muscovado sugar
juice of 1 small orange
2 tbsp olive oil

650g assorted tomatoes, cut into
   wedges and chunks
175g Pepperdew peppers in olive oil,
   drained
handful of small fresh basil leaves

1. Put the onion, sugar and orange juice in a bowl, toss together and set aside for 15 minutes, until the sugar dissolves and the onion softens. Stir in the oil.
2. Toss the tomatoes, peppers, basil and onion dressing together and serve at room temperature.

If you can't find Pepperdew sweet pickled peppers, use roasted red peppers in oil.

Orange & watercress salad

Serves 4–6

4 oranges, preferably navel or
　Valencia
6 spring onions
175g watercress
2 heads chicory, broken into leaves
6 tbsp extra-virgin olive oil
salt and freshly ground black pepper

1. Using a small sharp knife, cut the top and bottom off an orange. Stand the orange on a chopping board and cut away the skin and pith, from top to bottom, in sections. Hold the orange over a bowl and cut out each segment between the membrane, letting the segment and juice fall into the bowl. Squeeze out the juice from the empty membrane. Repeat for all the oranges.
2. Strain off and reserve the juice. Put the segments into a serving bowl. Trim the spring onions and finely shred into lengths. Add to the orange segments with the watercress and chicory.
3. Take 2 tbsp of the orange juice and whisk in the oil and plenty of seasoning in a small bowl. Drizzle over the salad and toss everything together and serve.

Watercress's peppery kick complements the citrus burst of fresh orange in this salad.

A rather old-fashioned rice salad

Serves 4

300g long-grain rice
100g podded broad beans
2 spring onions, sliced
200g can tuna steak in olive oil, drained
200g freshly grated Gruyère cheese
4 ripe tomatoes, deseeded and chopped
8 pickled cornichons
8 baby artichoke hearts in oil
100g radishes, trimmed, washed and sliced
4 tbsp extra-virgin olive oil
juice of 1 lemon
4 tbsp chopped fresh flat-leaf parsley, to garnish
salt and freshly ground black pepper

1. Wash the rice and put in a small saucepan with 450ml cold water. Cook for 15 minutes then spread the rice out over a baking tray and allow it to cool thoroughly.

2. In a large pan of salted, boiling water quickly blanch the broad beans for about 2 minutes, then shuck them from their skins by squeezing them between your thumb and forefinger.

3. Mix the broad beans, spring onions and rice in a large bowl. Fold in the tuna, cheese, tomatoes, cornichons, artichokes and radishes.

4. Whisk the olive oil with the lemon juice and fold into the salad. Season to taste and garnish with parsley to serve.

Country-style potato salad

Serves 6

550g waxy new potatoes, such as
  Pink Fir Apple or Charlotte
juice of ½ lemon
4 tbsp extra-virgin olive oil
2 tbsp chopped fresh oregano
1 small red onion, finely chopped

12 pitted green olives
4 plum tomatoes, deseeded and
  roughly chopped
2 tbsp capers
4 eggs, hard-boiled
salt and freshly ground black pepper

1. Cook the potatoes in boiling salted water for 12–15 minutes, until just tender. Drain well and cut in half. Put into a large bowl.

2. In a small bowl, whisk together 1 tbsp of lemon juice, the olive oil, oregano and plenty of seasoning. Pour over the warm potatoes and set aside.

3. When the potato salad has cooled, add the onion, olives, tomatoes and capers and toss well. Peel and roughly chop the boiled eggs and scatter over the salad. Toss the salad once more just before serving.

The addition of chopped eggs makes this a lovely alternative to a traditional potato salad.

Italian bean salad

Serves 4–6

7 tbsp extra-virgin olive oil

1 small onion, finely chopped

2 plump garlic cloves, crushed

1 stick celery, finely chopped

2 red chillies, deseeded and chopped

2 tsp chopped fresh oregano

410g can cannellini beans, drained and rinsed

410g can borlotti beans, drained and rinsed

6 plump tomatoes, deseeded and chopped

3 tbsp chopped fresh parsley

2 tbsp lemon juice

salt and freshly ground black pepper

1. Heat 3 tbsp of the olive oil in a large saucepan and cook the onion, garlic, celery and red chilli gently over a low heat for 6–8 minutes, until softened.

2. Stir in the oregano and all the beans and heat gently for 5–6 minutes, stirring occasionally. Remove from the heat and allow to cool.

3. Stir in the tomatoes and parsley. Whisk the remaining olive oil with the lemon juice and season well. Just before serving, pour over the bean mixture and toss well.

Serve this with smoky barbecued steaks, cold poached salmon or with a large mixed green salad.

Roasted baby beetroot

Serves 4

1 tsp caraway seeds (optional)

800g baby beetroot with tops

4 tbsp extra-virgin olive oil

1 tbsp balsamic or sherry vinegar

1 tbsp Dijon mustard

1 tsp sea salt

1. If you're using the caraway seeds, dry-toast in a hot pan for 30 seconds. Crush and set aside.

2. If the beetroot comes with the tops (greens), remove, wash, then blanch them for a minute in boiling water. Drain and set aside.

3. Preheat the oven to 220°C (fan 200°C), gas 7. Put the beetroot in a baking tray and toss with half the oil and a little salt. Roast for 20 minutes, until cooked through. When cooled slightly, put on clean rubber gloves and rub the beetroot skins off.

4. Whisk the remaining oil with the vinegar, mustard, caraway seeds and sea salt, then toss with the beetroot tops and roots.

If you store this in a covered container in the fridge, it keeps well for up to 2 days.

Fresh Italian parsley salad

Illustrated on the following pages

Serves 6
50g couscous
2 sun-dried tomatoes, finely chopped
2 tbsp olive oil
grated zest and juice of 1 lemon
25g black olives, pitted and finely
   chopped
50g fresh flat-leaf parsley leaves
salt and freshly ground black pepper

1. Put the couscous and sun-dried tomatoes in a large heat-proof bowl and pour over 50ml boiling water. Leave to cool.
2. Stir in the olive oil, lemon zest and juice, olives and some seasoning. Toss through the parsley just before serving.

You can make the couscous and tomato dressing earlier in the day but don't mix in the fresh parsley. Put it into a bowl with the parsley leaves on top, then cover and chill. Bring back to room temperature, then simply toss the parsley through to serve.

Christmas coleslaw

Serves 6–8

200g mayonnaise (see the recipe on
   page 278)
150g natural yogurt
1 tsp ground cumin
500g mixed sweet and crunchy
   salad, or mixed shredded white
   cabbage and carrot

50g toasted pecan nuts, roughly
   chopped
salt and freshly ground black pepper

1. In a serving bowl mix together the mayonnaise, yogurt and cumin.
Season to taste.

2. Add the mixed salad and toss well to coat in the dressing.

3. Just before serving, top with the pecan nuts.

A lovely rich slaw with a slight kick – ideal to
accompany cold meats.

Cool garden salad

Serves 6
1 English round crisp lettuce
¼ cucumber
1 small pomegranate
150g natural yogurt
3 tbsp chopped fresh mint
few dashes of Tabasco
2 tbsp white-wine vinegar

1. Wash the whole lettuce, then shake off the excess water. Cut off the base of the stalk, open up the lettuce and separate out the leaves. Arrange on a large serving platter.
2. Peel the cucumber and cut in half lengthways. Using a teaspoon, scrape out the seeds and discard. Thinly slice the cucumber and scatter the pieces over the lettuce.
3. Roll the pomegranate between your hands. Halve, hold upside-down and tap with a rolling pin to pop out the seeds. Sprinkle over the leaves.
4. Mix the yogurt, mint, Tabasco and vinegar together. Pour into a jug and drizzle over the salad to serve.

Carrot & cumin coleslaw

Serves 8

1 large onion, thinly sliced

2 large carrots, roughly grated

½ small white cabbage, finely sliced

1 tbsp cumin seeds

6 tbsp mayonnaise (see the recipe
  on page 278)

1 tbsp lemon juice

salt and freshly ground black pepper

1. Put the onion, carrots and cabbage in a big bowl and toss well. Set aside.
2. Toast the seeds in a dry pan over a medium heat for 1 minute, or until
aromatic. Cool slightly, then add to the vegetables with the mayonnaise and
lemon juice. Season and mix well.

salads
fruit

Orchard pudding

Serves 4

2 apples
2 pears
3 large plums
juice of 1 orange
1 generous tbsp sharp jam
  (e.g. quince preserve)

1 tbsp caster sugar
150ml Madeira wine or sweet sherry
300g Madeira cake or loaf of stale
  white bread, crusts removed and
  cut into thin slices
crème fraîche, to serve

1. Line a medium-sized pudding basin (about 1-litre capacity) with clingfilm and press firmly into the base and the sides. Leave enough overhanging the edges to cover the top later.

2. Peel, core and slice the apples and pears. Stone and roughly chop the plums. Pop all the fruit into a saucepan with the orange juice, jam and sugar. Stir everything together and bring to a simmer over a gentle heat. Cover and cook for about 10 minutes, or until the fruit is soft but still holding its shape. Allow it to cool completely in the juices.

3. Dilute the Madeira wine with about 3 tbsp of the cooled fruit juices and, one-by-one, briefly dunk each slice of cake or bread in the liquid. Starting at the base, line the inside of the pudding basin with the slices of bread, as for a summer pudding. Fill with the fruit and top with more cake or bread to enclose it completely. Wrap the overhanging clingfilm over the top, and cover with a weighted flat-based bowl or plate. Leave for at least 3 hours, or preferably overnight.

4. Peel back the clingfilm and invert the bowl over a serving dish. If the pudding doesn't slide out easily, tap the base with a wooden spoon. Serve with the crème fraîche.

This is a seasonal spin on the traditional summer pudding with a trifle-like texture.

Cherry & fig compote for ice cream

Serves 2
150ml port
1 small cinnamon stick
½ vanilla pod
1 rounded tbsp soft brown sugar
250g fresh cherries
2 fresh figs
good quality vanilla ice cream,
    to serve

1. Place the port in a pan with the cinnamon, vanilla and sugar and simmer over a low heat for 2–3 minutes, until reduced by about half.
2. Meanwhile, remove the stones from the cherries using a cherry or olive stoner and cut the figs into quarters.
3. Add the cherries to the pan and cook for 2 minutes, then add the figs and cook for a further minute. Remove from the heat and allow to cool slightly before serving with scoops of ice cream.

Orange & passion fruit with cardamom syrup

Illustrated on the previous pages

Serves 4–5
5 large oranges
75g golden caster sugar
5 cardamom pods, lightly crushed
5–6 passion fruit, halved
1–2 tbsp lemon juice
1–2 tbsp orange flower water

1. Thinly pare the zest of one orange using a potato peeler making sure that you include no white pith. Cut the strips into thin shreds, place in a sieve and pour a kettleful of boiling water over them. Leave to drain.
2. Place the caster sugar in a small pan with 4 tbsp of water and the crushed cardamom pods. Heat slowly until the sugar has melted, then leave it to boil for 2–3 minutes.
3. Scoop the passion fruit pulp into the syrup with the strips of orange zest and stir well to break up the passion fruit. Allow the mixture to cool. Add a little lemon juice to taste.
4. Peel all the oranges, removing the white pith and cut into thin slices. Arrange on a deep plate or platter and spoon the syrup over. Chill until ready to serve, then sprinkle with the orange-flower water.

This is exquisite served with cardamom ice cream or with a mixture of whipped cream and Greek yogurt.

Pineapple, passion fruit & pomegranate

Illustrated on the following pages

Serves 6

8 passion fruit
4 tbsp golden caster sugar
4 tbsp Malibu
1 pineapple, peeled, cored and
  halved lengthways
1 long red chilli, deseeded
handful small fresh mint leaves
1 pomegranate, halved

1. Halve the passion fruit and scoop the pulp out into a sieve resting over a saucepan. Use the back of a spoon to rub the pulp through the sieve to extract as much of the juice as possible. Discard the seeds.
2. Add the sugar and Malibu to the passion fruit juice and simmer over a medium heat for 3–5 minutes, until syrupy. Set aside to cool, or cover and chill overnight.
3. Sit a pineapple half cut-side down on a chopping board. Finely slice into semi-circles, then repeat with the other half. Arrange the pineapple slices in a circle on each serving plate.
4. Slice the chilli into very fine long slivers, then scatter over the pineapple along with some mint. Sit the pomegranate halves cut-side down on a chopping board and hit them several times with a rolling pin to release the seeds. Scatter the seeds over the pineapple and drizzle with the Malibu syrup just before serving.

This tropical winter dessert offers a lighter finish to dinner with pineapple, passion fruit, hot chilli and pomegranate seeds.

Citrus salad

Serves 2

2 limes

2 oranges

2 pink grapefruit

2 tbsp chopped fresh mint

a little honey, to drizzle

1. Remove the peel and pith from the limes, oranges and pink grapefruit. Slice into bite-sized pieces, reserving any juices that come from the fruit.
2. Put all the fruit in a serving dish and mix with the chopped mint and reserved juice. Drizzle with a little honey, to serve.

This light, refreshing salad is the perfect ending to a rich meal.

Autumn fruit salad

Illustrated on the following pages

Serves 6

500g ripe plums or greengages,
   washed and stalks removed
2–3 ripe peaches or nectarines
2 ripe dessert pears
150g fresh blackberries

For the syrup

110g golden granulated sugar
1 stick cinnamon
1 large lemon
2–3 thin slices fresh ginger

1. Start by making the syrup. Place the sugar and 150ml of water in a pan.
Add the cinnamon stick, two or three pieces of the pared lemon rind and the
sliced ginger. Stir over a low heat until the sugar has dissolved, then bring
to a simmer. Remove from the heat and leave to infuse until cold.

2. Squeeze the lemon and add the juice to the syrup, then strain it into a
large serving bowl.

3. Now prepare the fruit. Cut the plums or greengages in half, following
their natural line, and remove the stones. Slice into fairly chunky pieces and
add to the spiced syrup.

4. Scald the peaches, remove the skins, then halve them. Remove the stones
and slice. There's no need to skin the nectarines, just halve them, remove the
stones and slice. Add these to the syrup, too.

5. Peel and halve the pears. Scoop out the cores using a teaspoon. Slice the
pears into quarters or eighths so you have long slivers, then add them to
the syrup as well. Turn them over so that they are fully coated in the lemon
juice to keep them white. Finally, add the blackberries.

6. Let everything marinate for 2–3 hours before serving – the syrup will
draw out the natural fruit juices to achieve a perfect balance of flavours.

This fruit salad is very versatile; it can be
served for dessert, with natural yogurt,
or spooned over muesli for breakfast.

Strawberries, liqueur & mascarpone cream

Serves 4

500g small strawberries, hulled and halved

2 tbsp Cointreau or orange liqueur

finely grated zest of ½ small orange

1 tbsp icing sugar, plus 1–2 tsp for the cream

5cm vanilla pod

125g mascarpone

2 tbsp single cream

1. Put the strawberries, Cointreau liqueur, orange zest and icing sugar in a bowl and mix together gently. Cover and chill in the fridge for about an hour, until the strawberry juices have run a little. Bring it back up to room temperature.

2. Just before serving, slit open the vanilla pod and scrape out the seeds. Mix with the mascarpone, cream and some extra icing sugar to taste.

3. Serve the strawberries in dessert glasses and top with a little of the mascarpone cream.

Tropical fruit crumble

Serves 6

2 bananas

2 tsp lemon juice

1 mango, flesh peeled and chopped

½ medium pineapple, peeled,
  core removed and chopped

2 satsumas, peeled and separated
  into segments

150ml freshly squeezed orange juice

1 tbsp clear honey

150g sugar-free muesli

50g cold unsalted butter, cut into
  cubes

50g whole blanched hazelnuts

To serve

500g Greek yogurt mixed with
  1 tbsp honey and pinch powdered
  cinnamon

1. Preheat the oven to 180°C (fan 170°C), gas 4. Peel and chop the bananas, and toss in a bowl with the lemon juice. Add the mango, pineapple, satsumas, orange juice and honey. Mix together gently.

2. Whiz the muesli and butter in a food processor for a couple of minutes. Add the nuts and whiz again – you want the nuts to remain chunky.

3. Tip the fruit into an 18–20cm-square ovenproof dish and scatter over the muesli mixture. Bake in the centre of the oven for 30 minutes (cover with foil if the top browns too much). Serve with the Greek yoghurt in a separate bowl to add as much as you like.

Spiced cherries in vodka

Serves 6
450g cherries, stalks left on
400ml cranberry juice
200ml vodka
200ml apple juice
50ml cherry brandy
1 tbsp juniper berries, crushed
pinch of ground allspice

1. Prick the cherries in several places with a sterilised needle so that they will absorb the vodka mixture better.
2. Mix all the remaining ingredients together in a large jug or bowl.
3. Add the pricked cherries, cover and set aside in a cool place for anything between 1–12 hours before serving up in shot glasses.

You can serve this after 1 hour of macerating but, obviously, the longer you leave it, the more potent it will become. You could use orange liqueur in place of the cherry brandy.

Pineapple with mint & lime sugar

Serves 4
1 large ripe, sweet pineapple
50g caster sugar
finely grated zest of 1 lime
large handful fresh mint leaves

1. Carefully slice the top and bottom off the pineapple. Stand it upright on a chopping board and slice away all the skin and the little brown 'eyes'. Quarter lengthways so you have four long wedges. Slice away the woody cores from each wedge.
2. Cut the pineapple across each wedge into thin slices and arrange them in small tumblers. Cover with clingfilm and chill in the fridge until needed.
3. To serve, put the sugar, lime zest and mint leaves into the bowl of a small food processor and blitz for about 30 seconds, until the mint is finely chopped and you have a bright green mixture. Sprinkle over the pineapple in each glass and serve.

Ripe pineapples smell sweet and the leaves should pull out quite easily from the centre. Don't be tempted to make the sugar before you need it because the mint will start to go black and lose its fresh taste.

salads
dressings
&
mayonnaise

French dressing

Serves 4

1 tbsp white-wine vinegar
1 tsp mild mustard (such as
    wholegrain or Dijon)
a small pinch of sugar
3 tbsp extra-virgin olive oil
salt and freshly ground black pepper

1. Put the white-wine vinegar, mustard, sugar and some seasoning into a large bowl. Whisk until well emulsified.
2. Add the extra-virgin olive oil in a slow, steady stream, whisking all the time, until cloudy and slightly thickened.

A good all-round dressing that is used throughout this book. It works well with all manner of ingredients, from chicken and steaks to smoked fish and mixed leaf salads.

Basil vinaigrette

Serves 4
6 tbsp extra-virgin olive oil
2 tbsp red-wine vinegar
15g torn basil leaves
1 small garlic clove
1 shallot, finely chopped
a pinch of sugar
salt and freshly ground black pepper

Put all the ingredients with some seasoning into the bowl of a small food processor and whiz until smooth.

A perfect addition to a simple salad of grilled fish, chicken or meat as well as tomato or new potato salads.

Poppy seed vinaigrette

Serves 4

1 tbsp poppy seeds
¼ tsp Dijon mustard
1 tbsp balsamic vinegar
3 tbsps olive oil
½ small shallot, finely chopped

1. Dry-fry the poppy seeds in a non-stick pan over a high heat for 1 minute, until lightly toasted.
2. In a small bowl, whisk the mustard with the balsamic vinegar then gradually whisk in the olive oil.
3. Add the seeds and the chopped shallot and stir well to mix together.

Use this dressing to liven up a bowl of green leaves. It is great on all leafy salads for adding a bit of crunch.

Lemon vinaigrette

Serves 4

3 tbsp extra-virgin olive oil
1 tbsp freshly squeezed lemon juice
salt and freshly ground black pepper

In a small bowl whisk the extra-virgin olive oil with the lemon juice,
adding a little seasoning to taste.

Brilliant for vegetable salads, such as broad
beans and Feta cheese, or beetroot.

Walnut oil dressing

Serves 4

3 tbsp walnut oil

4 tbsp extra-virgin olive oil

2 tbsp white wine vinegar

1 tsp golden caster sugar

Combine all of the ingredients in a small, lidded jar and shake together.

Walnut oil has a strong, distinct flavour and requires a hearty salad to stand up to it. Beetroot, goats' cheese and meat salads are excellent choices for this dressing.

Mediterranean dressing

Serves 4

100g marinated sundried peppers in olive oil, plus 2 tbsp of the oil from the jar

3 tbsp lemon juice

3 tbsp olive oil

1 tsp dijon mustard

10 basil leaves

6 pitted Kalamata or other black olives

1 heaped tbsp capers, drained

6–8 tbsp boiling water to loosen

salt and freshly ground black pepper

1. Put the peppers along with their oil, the lemon juice, olive oil and the dijon mustard into the bowl of a small food processor or blender and whizz for 20–30 seconds or until smooth. Season to taste. Turn into a mixing bowl.
2. Chop the capers and olives and shred the basil leaves and add to the bowl. Stir together adding the hot water gradually until the mixture has loosened to the right consistency.

Use as a dressing for roasted vegetables, couscous or new potato salads.

Classic Caesar dressing

Serves 4
1 large garlic clove
1 anchovy fillet
1 egg yolk
¼ tsp Dijon mustard

1 tbsp lemon juice
100ml mild olive oil
2 tbsp grated Parmesan
½ tbsp double cream
freshly ground black pepper

1. Crush the garlic clove under the blade of a large knife and rub it around the inside of a bowl, then discard.

2. Mash the anchovy fillet on a board with the blade of a knife and add to the bowl. Add the egg yolk, mustard and lemon juice. Whisk until smooth.

3. Slowly whisk in the olive oil, until creamy. Stir in the grated Parmesan, double cream and some pepper.

To make a Caesar salad, toss lettuce leaves in the dressing and scatter with shaved Parmesan to serve (see the recipe on page 24).

Blue cheese dressing

Serves 4

50g blue cheese (Gorgonzola is good)
2 tbsp milk
1 tbsp white-wine vinegar
6 tbsp olive oil
salt and freshly ground black pepper

Put the cheese in the bowl of a food processor along with the milk, white-wine vinegar, olive oil and a little seasoning; blend until smooth. Add a few drops of warm water if it seems a little thick.

Serve over a crunchy salad of watercress, avocado and peppery radish.

Mayonnaise

Serves 4–6
2 medium egg yolks
1 tsp Dijon mustard
300ml light olive oil
good squeeze fresh lemon juice
salt and freshly ground black pepper

1. Sit a large bowl on a cloth to stop it moving. Put the egg yolks into the bowl along with the Dijon mustard and a little seasoning and whisk well until smooth.
2. Gradually add the olive oil in a slow, steady stream, whisking all the time. You should have a smooth, quite thick mayonnaise that stands in peaks.
3. Add lemon juice to taste and briefly whisk. If it's too thick, whisk in a few drops of warm water to give a good consistency.

This will keep, covered, in the fridge for 3–4 days.

Aïoli

Serves 6–8
6 garlic cloves, crushed
3 egg yolks
3 tbsp fresh white breadcrumbs
4 tbsp white-wine vinegar
300ml good olive oil
salt and freshly ground black pepper

1. Put the garlic cloves, egg yolks, breadcrumbs, white-wine vinegar and a little seasoning into a bowl and whisk well (or whiz in a food processor).
2. Gradually whisk in the olive oil in a slow, steady trickle (or pour through the funnel of the food processor with the motor still running).
3. Whisk in 1 tbsp warm water and check the seasoning.

Serve as a dip with fresh crudités – as well as the usual carrot sticks and celery, try strips of fennel, asparagus and radishes. Combine with cooked potatoes to create a garlicky potato salad, or use as a sauce for fish and shellfish.

Acknowledgements

Most of the recipes in this book were first published in **delicious.** magazine or **Sainsbury's Magazine**. We are thankful to all the staff (past and present) involved in both magazines and to those at the Seven Publishing Group for providing the material and their assistance.

Recipes by:

Felicity Barnum-Bobb
24 Classic Caesar salad; 86 Tuna and pesto pasta salad; 257 Spiced cherries in vodka

Fiona Beckett
156 Pheasant, apple, fennel and orange salad

Kate Belcher
15 Broad bean, mint and crispy pancetta; 32 Crab, avocado & crispy bacon salad; 67 Nicoise salad of bacon and cheesy croûtons; 73 Minted lamb kebabs with bean & rocket; 101 Sweet chilli prawn and egg noodle salad; 130 Chicken and mango with chilli lime dressing; 152 Chinese duck, orange and noodle salad; 178 Roasted baby vegetable salad with croûtons; 188 Runner bean, tomato and pesto salad; 264 French dressing; 266 Basil vinaigrette; 269 Poppy seed vinaigrette; 270 Lemon vinaigrette; 274 Classic Caesar dressing; 277 Blue cheese dressing; 278 Mayonnaise

Angela Boggiano
23 Zesty herb and chilli crab salad with crostini; 33 Sticky spare ribs and crunchy slaw; 198 Salad with toasted mixed seeds

Lorna Brash
64 Paprika spiced pork; 147 Thai chicken salad

Tamsin Burnett-Hall
112 Warm salad of smoked salmon and pancetta; 228 Christmas coleslaw

Matthew Drennan
12 Parma ham, fig and mozzarella salad; 17 Vietnamese salad; 48 Seared steak, mango and radish salad; 50 Hot Thai beef salad; 68 Apple and pork salad with cider dressing; 72 Ham with peach and couscous; 74 Warm Sunday roast salad; 85 Seared tuna with bean and olive salad; 96 Prawn, orange and fennel salad; 115 Peppered mackerel with vegetable crisps; 126 Warm chicken, tomato, Feta and lemon salad; 138 Chicken with croûtons and Gorgonzola dressing; 140 Moroccan chicken and potato salad; 143 Chicken and crunchy tortilla salad; 144 Warm chicken with tarragon mayonnaise; 148 Vietnamese minted chicken salad; 166 Couscous, broad beans, peas, mint and Feta; 168 Mediterranean vegetable salad; 170 New potato, sun-dried tomato and olive salad; 176 Greek salad; 194 Herb leaf salad; 195 Red cabbage and beetroot salad;

216 Orange and watercress salad; 220 Country-style potato salad; 222 Italian bean salad; 232 Carrot and cumin coleslaw; 282 Aioli

Silvana Franco
107 Seafood salad with lime and chilli salsa; 213 Tomato and sweet pickled pepper salad; 225 Fresh Italian parsley salad

Brian Glover
103 Sweet potato, orange and mussel salad; 136 Chicken noodle salad with ginger and peanuts; 244 Orange and passion fruit with cardamom syrup

Angela Hartnett
30 Goats' cheese and beetroot salad

Ghillie James
20 All-day breakfast salad; 52 Griddled steak with potatoes and peppers; 62 Sicilian sausages with lentils; 92 Tuna salad with beans, capers & new potatoes; 106 Crab, avocado and pink grapefruit salad; 118 Haddock, crispy bacon and spinach salad; 182 Griddled vegetables with mozzarella; 208 New potatoes with chorizo and broad beans; 272 Walnut oil dressing

Jennifer Joyce
53 Warm new potato and smoked sausage salad; 76 Lamb and aubergine with pomegranate; 149 Five-spice duck salad with chicory and pears; 199 Warm barley salad with butternut squash

Debbie Major
58 Warm potato salad with Parma ham; 82 Tuna, fennel and white bean salad; 127 Smoked chicken and papaya salad; 209 Braised peas with leeks, lettuces and mint; 252 Strawberries, liqueur and mascarpone cream; 258 Pineapple with mint and lime sugar

Kim Morphew
90 Chargrilled pesto tuna with potato salad; 134 Crispy chilli chicken salad; 230 Cool garden salad

Tom Norrington-Davies
26 Tomato, peach and cumin salad; 34 Squid, lemon and caper salad; 37 Warm salad of pear, scallop and chorizo; 44 Tagliata (seared steak and rocket salad); 98 Strawberry and langoustine salad; 102 Razor clams and blood oranges; 154 Spiced pigeon with roast butternut squash;

173 Roast pepper and garlic salad with hazelnuts; 174 Mangetout and avocado salad; 180 Grilled spring onions, radish and cottage cheese; 202 Courgette som tam; 210 Warm pea and lentil salad; 219 A rather old-fashioned rice salad; 224 Roasted baby beetroot; 238 Orchard pudding

Sarah Randell
28 Coriander and coconut crab salad; 16 Warm chicken and herb salad; 47 Griddled beef salad with mushrooms; 59 BLT salad; 93 Prawn, watercress and spinach salad; 116 Herring with potato, beetroot and dill salad; 124 Chicken, red onion and green beans; 133 Chicken, asparagus and avocado salad; 172 Potato, watercress & apple salad; 248 Citrus salad; 254 Tropical fruit crumble

Annie Rigg
22 Tomato, fresh mint & lemon salad; 88 Tuna and cannellini bean salad; 110 Smoked fish salad; 240 Cherry and fig compote for ice cream

Natalie Seldon
57 Warm mozzarella, bacon and nectarine

Linda Tubby
162 Warm spinach, shallot and baby beetroot salad; 165 Little Gem, mushroom, apple and celery salad; 185 Five bean salad with shallot and quails' eggs; 204 Hot potato, orange and red cabbage salad

Mitzie Wilson
38 Chicory and apple salad

Photography credits:
Steve Baxter 18–19, 39, 108-109, 132, 141, 167, 169, 177, 196–197, 214–215, 217, 221, 223, 226-227; Peter Cassidy 21, 29, 46, 49, 54-55, 77, 150–151, 200–201, 206–207; Jean Cazals 246–247; Lisa Cohen 94-95; Gus Filgate 250–251; Ewan Francis 49; Jonathan Gregson 128-129, 218; Janine Hosegood 75; Richard Jung 14, 60–61, 117, 125, 189, 253; Andrew Montgomery 31; Gareth Morgans 69, 91, 100, 114, 135, 153, 179; Lis Parsons 65, 56, 66, 83, 146, 171, 231, 233, 256, 255; Michael Paul 104–105, 137, 163, 164, 186–187, 205, 242-243, 259; Claire Richards 25, 87; Deidre Rooney 13, 51, 70–71, 84, 145; Clive Streeter 119, 131, 183; Lucinda Symons 283; Lucinda Symons and Anthony Blake pic. Library 265, 267, 268, 271, 275, 276, 279-281; Peter Thiedeke 97, 139, 142; Simon Walton 89, 111, 113, 229, 241; Cameron Watt 157; Rob White 27, 35, 36, 45, 99, 155, 175, 181, 203, 211, 239.